# Honey Bees

Letters from the Hive

# Honey Bees

## Letters from the Hive

### Stephen Buchmann

Delacorte Press

All rights reserved. Published in the United States by Delacorte Press,
an imprint of Random House Children's Books, a division of
Random House, Inc., New York.

Delacorte Press is a registered trademark and the colophon
is a trademark of Random House, Inc.

This work is based upon *Letters from the Hive:*
*An Intimate History of Bees, Honey, and Humankind*
by Stephen Buchmann with Banning Repplier, published by Bantam,
an imprint of the Random House Publishing Group,
a division of Random House, Inc.,
New York, in 2005.

Visit us on the Web! www.randomhouse.com/teens

Educators and librarians, for a variety of teaching tools,
visit us at www.randomhouse.com/teachers

Library of Congress Cataloging-in-Publication Data is available upon request.

ISBN 978-0-385-73770-8 (hc) — ISBN 978-0-385-90683-8 (lib. bdg.) —
ISBN 978-0-375-89557-9 (e-book)

The text of this book is set in 11-point Century Schoolbook.

Book design by Cathy Boback

Printed in the United States of America
10 9 8 7 6 5 4 3 2 1
First Edition

# Contents

# Honey Bees

## Letters from the Hive

Dedicated to "Pak Teh," a fine friend,
for sharing rituals during many Malaysian honey hunts.
With fondest memories . . .

Salleh bin Mohammed Noor
(Jitra, Kedah Province)
(1925–2009)

# Chapter 1
# Secrets of the Bee:
# Abuzz with Activity

## Oh, to Be a Bee!

HONEY BEES LIVE in a world vastly different from ours. On a fresh spring morning a bee looks down on fields of colorful wildflowers through many-faceted compound eyes. A bee has five compound eyes, each with thousands of slender hairs growing from its surface. Through these hairy eyes, one would see vibrant colors and rapid movements inaccessible to the sensory powers of human beings.

While life on the wing could be magical, it would not be without risk. A bee could unwittingly fly into the snare of an orb-weaver spider's web or, ironically, find itself trapped in the folds of an entomologist's aerial net, condemned to the bitter-almond vapors of the killing jar.

Honey bees savor tastes ranging from sweet to sour and back again, not only through cells in their mouth but also through sensitive hairs on their antennae. Bees would smell not through a big, protuberant nose but through thousands of minute sensory pits scattered across the surface of their antennae. This is called olfaction and is extremely important for bees. Without it, bees wouldn't be able to locate flowers as easily, recognize nest mates, smell an intruder in the colony, detect alarm pheromones given off by colleagues who have spotted danger. Floral scents cling to bees' hairy wax-covered bodies as insistently as the scent of a woman's perfume clings to a man's jacket after dancing close. When bees return to the hive after a successful foraging trip, the clinging fragrances inform their sisters of the kinds of blossoms they've visited during the day, a sort of travel log recording forays into floral landscapes, or bee pastures. More importantly, these scents help direct new recruits to the best sources of nectar and pollen.

The scents of the outside world don't mask the unique scent of the home nest, which is always there to serve as an olfactory identity badge. Guard bees sniff the body odor of workers returning from the field; if they smell something unfamiliar, the stranger is kept out or even attacked and killed if it persists in trying to enter.

## Home Sweet Home: Life in the Hive

If we could shrink ourselves down to bee size and enter the inner world of the nest, we would find it an alien place, dark, crowded, and oppressively hot and humid. But bees are not humans, and presumably they feel comfortable in the hive, which is home to a queen, tens of thousands of her daughters (sterile worker bees), and a few hundred or so of her sons, the drones. Double-sided hexagonal combs hang like graceful parallel curtains from the ceiling of the hive. Like large corporations that house thousands of employees in diminutive side-by-side cubicles, the beeswax nest is a highly compartmented and efficient workplace. The waxen cubicles serve a multitude of functions, from honey and pollen storage pantries and larval nurseries to dance floors for the waggle dancing of returning foragers.

*A tangle of worker bee bodies. The honey bee nest is a crowded place.*

Waggle dancing is one of nature's most fascinating means of communication. When a successful forager returns from the field with a special stomach (the crop) full of nectar or bulging hind-leg pollen baskets, she performs a lively dance on the vertical combs—a little wagtail movement followed by a straight upward run—that imparts information to the bees watching and listening to the show. The spectators routinely beg for a sip of nectar from the obliging dancer, who takes a break to pass out free samples.

Karl von Frisch, an Austrian animal behaviorist who shared a Nobel Prize in physiology and medicine in 1973, spent decades studying what he called the "dance language of the honey bees." Von Frisch determined that the straight-run portion of the waggle dance indicated the direction of the floral patch, while the vigor of the waggling, accompanied by pulsed buzzing vibrations, imparted the relative distance to the food. Dancing straight up on the combs indicated that the recruited bees should fly toward the sun to find the correct flowers. If the food was located in the opposite direction of the sun, the performer danced straight down on the combs of the nest. Odors also play a primary role in how bees locate and remember flowers. Foragers return to their nests with the lively scents of flowers clinging to their hairy bodies. Other bees smell these scents and it helps them to locate and recognize them far from the nest.

Beeswax, the building material of the hive's interior, is biochemically expensive to make. It takes almost twenty pounds of honey, digested and biochemically transformed in the bees' bodies (wax glands), to produce just one pound of the precious wax. This is why beekeepers often supply ready-made beeswax foundation sheets to their colonies—they'd rather have this honey for their own use, saving the bees some effort. Beeswax is secreted by eight paired glands under the abdomen of the bee, then chewed and softened until it is pliable enough to be shaped into the thin-walled hexagonal cells of the combs.

How the geometric combs are constructed by the workers without a supervisor, blueprints, rulers, or protractors remains a mystery. Previously, scientists believed that the precision of the hexagonal cells was the result of an instinctive behavior that stimulated the bees to add, remove, and fashion the wax in just the right way to ensure that the walls and angles were all perfectly aligned. Recently, it has been suggested that the hexagonal cells are an "emergent property," that is, at the right temperature (between 37 and 40°C), the hexagons form on their own. First the bees make cylindrical tubes around themselves and then the hexagonal angles form. Chemically, the beeswax transforms from an amorphous (or unorganized) state into a crystalline state. As strange as this sounds, look at the angles where soap bubbles touch one another to form 120-degree angles. Or roll out some clay cylinders the thickness of a pencil with your hands. Take ten or so and wrap them in a cardboard sleeve. Squeeze them together slowly. You get hexagons! Hexagons are found in other examples of animal architecture, like wasp nests or under the sea in the hard limey skeletons of corals.

## The Queen and Her Consorts

The drones follow a seductive chemical pheromone trail released by queens, who are virgins and ready to mate. A healthy queen mates with seven to ten drones on a given mating flight. She may make a number of mating flights over the course of several subsequent days.

Two to four days after her mating flights, the queen returns to the colony, which she will never leave again, to begin her new role as an egg layer. A longer version of her daughters, with an elongated abdomen, she can lay up to fifteen hundred eggs a day throughout her life of one to three years, for a possible grand total of six hundred thousand progeny. When she's ready to lay, the queen walks over the surface of the combs in the brood nest, the central part of the nest, searching for empty cells that have been cleaned. When she finds an acceptable cell, she backs into it and lays a single, brilliant white egg, then backs out and moves on—a task that is repeated hundreds of times a day, every day of her life, except during the winter.

Not surprisingly, the queen receives preferential treatment in the colony, the very survival of which depends on her. A retinue of her daughters makes sure she is always fed and well groomed. Despite all the attention, however, the life of this "royal" is a lot more work than play or idle time. But did you know that bees sleep? They take little "bee naps" almost any time of day or night.

*A queen honey bee is surrounded by her daughters, the worker bees of the colony.*

## The Making of a Worker Bee: Egg to Adult in Twenty-one Days

Once the queen has deposited a fertilized egg in its cell, the female larva develops rapidly and hatches in only three days. As soon as the larva hatches from the egg, it begins feeding on a milky white secretion, called royal jelly, secreted by young females known as nurse bees. The larvae are insatiable, always hungry, their only imperative to grow as fast as they possibly can. Whitish, legless grublike creatures, they look nothing like the bees they will become. Their heads are very small, and they have no eyes, antennae, wings, or stingers. They do, however, have jaws, mandibles, and a mouth through which all that food passes.

The hexagonal brood cells are left open during most of the larval development. This allows the nurse bees to make thousands of cell inspections and deposit more food as needed. The future female workers, like the future male drones, receive royal jelly for the first three days and are then fed a mixture of pollen and nectar known as bee bread. Larvae from fertilized eggs destined to become queens are fed exclusively on royal jelly during their entire sixteen-day development.

*Worker bee standing on top of, and tending, the "bee bread" (stored pollen) for the colony.*

On the ninth day of their lives, when they have finished eating their bee bread, the worker larvae become rigid, with their heads facing out of the cell openings. From tiny paired openings near their mouths, they spin brownish silk for their cocoons, getting ready for the short but internally dynamic stage called the pupa, which is anything but rest even though the pupae are mostly immobile.

From day eleven to day twenty, the tissues of the pupa

develop into the flesh of the adult bee. The eyes turn pink, then chocolate brown, and finally black. Like a monarch butterfly inside its chrysalis, the larva's body is undergoing an amazing series of changes.

Finally, on the twenty-first day, a new female worker bee emerges, chewing her way through the cell cap. Male drones, after undergoing similar development, emerge on the twenty-fourth day, while queens emerge after only sixteen days. The female "newbies" are paler than their older siblings and look a bit like wet dogs. Over the course of several hours, their hairs dry and fluff out and their skin hardens and darkens (called tanning), making them look more like mature adults. Soon they figure out how to walk, using the versatile "tripod" stance of all insects—three legs off the ground and three on.

As she ages, the female worker bee will have many different job descriptions. She begins adult life as a nurse bee, charged with feeding larvae and cleaning cells. Then, as she matures, she progresses to honey maker and will take on other tasks around the nest, such as making new wax cells and tending the queen. Finally she will take flight, emerging from the nest to forage for nectar and pollen far from the safety of home. If she emerges as a new adult during the spring or summer months, chances are she will live for only four to six weeks—a brief, exhausting, but highly productive life. Each worker may make from four to ten or so flights from the nest each day, visiting hundreds or many thousands of flowers to collect nectar and pollen. During her lifetime, a worker bee may have flown from 35,000 to 55,000 miles collecting food for her and her nest mates! One pound of honey stored in the comb can represent 200,000 miles of combined bee flights and nectar from as many as five million flowers. Did you know that honey bee foragers get great "gas mileage"? Bees can travel 4.7 million miles for every gallon of honey they eat. Of course, they actually have much smaller "gas tanks." Each forager brings back about fifty times as much energy as the flight costs.

Unlike his busy sisters, the drone has only one job, to mate with the queen and donate his genes to her stored sperm for the eventual production of new females. Once his task has been completed, his life's work is done, and, without further ado, he simply dies.

## "Queen Substance": The Foundation of Royal Power

Pheromones are sex-attractant chemicals given off by many insect species. In the case of honey bees, these chemicals, produced solely by the queens, are called queen substance. At county fairs across the United States, savvy beekeepers tie caged queens, or synthetic pheromone lures, under their chins to attract workers into a seething "bee beard," an alarming spectacle that never fails to impress the amazed crowd.

Not only is queen substance a powerful love potion, it also helps maintain the social structure of the colony. Thanks to its allure, worker bees flock to their mother to tend to her every need. Young, vigorous queens produce great quantities of queen substance, but the level gradually wanes as the queen ages. This decrease in production may spark a supersedure, or coup d'état, by the worker bees, who replace the old queen with a younger one. When a queen dies or is removed by the beekeeper to start a new colony, the disappearance of queen substance from the nest stimulates the workers to produce enlarged cells, stocked with plenty of royal jelly, in order to rear several new aspirants to the throne. If the aspirants emerge at the same time, they fight to the death, and the survivor becomes the new queen. If one emerges before the others, she eliminates her rivals by stinging them to death while they are still in their cells. In reality, the queen isn't in charge, the workers are!

# Chapter 2
# Flowers and Bees: The Dance

MOST PEOPLE REALIZE that there is an association between flowers and bees, and other pollinators, that plays an essential role in their reproduction. The bee familiar to most of us is the European honey bee, in the genus *Apis,* of tropical origin. It sips the nectar that flowers secrete to attract and reward pollinating insects. The nectar is a sugary bribe in return for pollination and the chance to collect the protein- and lipid-rich pollen grains as solid food. Back at the nest, the bees concentrate the nectar, adding sugar-splitting enzymes, then ripen and store it in capped hexagonal beeswax combs. Once eaten, the sugars in nectar and honey fuel their flight and, as the nutrients are metabolized, keep the colony warm during long, temperate-zone winters.

Though we joke about the birds and the bees, to experience a day in the life of a bee, we will take an incredible journey—seeing the world as the bees experience it and learning the secrets of their interactions with the many flowers they visit in the course of a busy day. It's an elaborate mating ritual and a desperate game of survival, for without bees, the world's quarter million flowering plant species could not procreate, and without the flowers, the bees would starve.

## Flower Parts

Flowers are living billboards, vying for pollinator attention. Our planet has more than a quarter million species of angiosperms, or flowering plants. Their blossoms call out in myriad sizes and shapes, exude nutritious oils and sweet, exotic, sometimes surprising scents, and display a dazzling array of color, the most saturated in nature. They brought life to our largely green and brown landscapes long before we were there to harvest, grow in a garden, or even take notice of them.

Flowers grow everywhere on land, from the frozen wastes of the Arctic tundra to rocky desert outcrops and luxuriant rain forest canopies. They are so common we often take them for granted. Some, such as yellow dandelions popping up in manicured green lawns, we think of as weeds and relentlessly strike down with herbicides and spades. But where would we be without public and private gardens, prom corsages and bridal bouquets, cut-flower centerpieces that enliven tables, meadows blanketed with wildflowers, and of course perfume?

## Pollination: A Lucky Accident

Pollination, the transfer of pollen grains from the male part of one flower (the anther) to the receptive female part of another (the stigma), is really nothing more than a lucky accident—lucky for us and the millions of animals with whom we share the planet. We depend on bees and other animal pollinators for 35 percent of our global food supply. Although wind-pollinated plants (cereals and grains) keep the planet's nearly seven billion people from starvation, it is the colorful and tasty fruits and vegetables that sustain and nurture us with life-giving nutrients and vitamins. These delicious products (apples, oranges, peaches, blueberries, etc.) were once flowers visited by bees and then became fruits. Besides, at least for me, pollinators help fill our pantries and refrigerators with the tastiest and healthiest foods. Our diets would be boring and bland if we ate only rice, wheat, or corn.

Flowering plants require pollination to reproduce, and pollination is a "lucky accident" because insects and other pollinating animals don't set out to do a daily good deed by spreading the pollen around. They are on a daily life-and-death search for food. For bees, pollen grains aren't the male gametes of flowering plants, but protein- and lipid-rich food that they depend on to nourish themselves and their hungry brood back at the nest.

Pollen grains are tiny, microscopic in fact, and sticky, and they come in all shapes and sizes. Most have oily surfaces, and many have spines or other textures. When bees zero in on a flower, pollen sticks to the feathery hairs that densely cover the bees' bodies. Electrostatic charges make the seal between bee and pollen all the tighter, because the pollen grains are negatively charged while bees acquire a strong positive charge during flight. Besides the pollen they inadvertently gather while buzzing about in the interior of a flower—the pollen that will fertilize other flowers—the bees also harvest pollen for their own purposes. Some of them, honey bees and bumble bees, moisten the harvested pollen with saliva, working it into a pliable mass attached to the smooth concave regions on their hind legs, the corbicula, or pollen baskets. Other bees carry dry pollen back to their nests, transported among the coarse mats of thick hair on their hind legs, or underneath their abdomens in the case of leafcutter and mason bees. *Diadasia enavata,* a sunflower-loving bee of the United States, is so laden with bright orange pollen by the time it finishes its work that it looks like a flying Cheetos snack as it heads for home.

## What's In It for Them: Floral Rewards That Keep Bees Coming Back for More

Flowering plants use bees and other pollinating animals as go-betweens to get their ovules fertilized, creating the seeds that germinate into new plants. As for the bees, they have a multitude of uses for the pollen and nectar they harvest from the flowers, ensuring that they will always be back for more. Pollen is the bees' primary source of food. Think of it as the beefsteak, or beans, the rich protein of the bees' diet. Nectar is also a crucial item on the bees' menu, especially honey bees, which use it for developing larvae and also as fuel, powering the flight muscles of adult bees as they visit their floral partners. In fact, honey bees are champion sugar addicts. The nectar they imbibe is from 30 to 50 percent sugar. Compare that to Coca-Cola, which is "only" 10 percent dissolved sugars.

Flowers don't freely give away all the pollen they produce as bee food just to be nice to pollinators! A few precious grains must get there on their own, in the wind, or ride piggyback on pollinators to find their tiny stigmatic targets; otherwise the whole pollination process would collapse. Obviously, both bees and flowers are getting what they need from the interchange, since the system of floral enticements traded for pollen special delivery has worked for millions of years, keeping flowers fertile, bees well fed, and our planet alive and green.

## Foraging for Nectar and Pollen

About 25 percent of a colony's worker population is comprised of mature females over the age of two or three weeks, which are responsible for gathering the raw materials upon which the colony depends for its survival. Honey bees have been known to fly as far as nine miles from their nests in search of pollen and nectar. Most often, however, they fly between one and three miles from home. If you draw a circle with a radius of several miles around a honey bee nest, you begin to appreciate just how much territory the colony requires to stock its waxen pantries. It has been estimated that foraging bees from one colony explore an area of 124 square miles in temperate regions and 186 in tropical forests to locate food and water.

Leaving the safety of the nest can be risky business. Wind currents and rainstorms can blow bees off course. Birds, lizards, robber flies, and crab spiders all lie in wait, ready to snare foragers to satisfy their own food needs.

Most foragers venture out of the nest about four to eight times a day. On each trip, a worker bee usually remains faithful to one kind of flowering plant. This constancy is good for the flowers because it means the bees transfer the pollen of one species only to other members of the same species. If bees routinely delivered the pollen of one species to the flowers of a different species, they would not be effective pollinators, and plant reproduction would suffer. Honey bees collect nectar in a special sac called the honey stomach, or crop. To get the job done efficiently, each worker comes equipped with a three-part interlocking structure, the bee tongue, or proboscis, extending from her mouth, which enables her to sip every last drop of sweet liquid from deep within blossoms.

The amount of bee labor and flight time that goes into making the honey sold in a typical sixteen-ounce jar at the supermarket is staggering to think about. The contents of that ordinary container represent the efforts of tens of thousands of bees flying a total of 112,000 miles to forage nectar from about 4.5 million flowers! *Note: See similar calculations on page 10.

# How Bees Make Honey

For centuries, it was assumed that honey bees simply visited flowers and collected the honey ready-made, bringing it back to the hive and storing it there. And calling honey "bee barf" or vomit, as some do for shock value, is also not accurate.

The truth is that honey making is an elaborate and complicated process. The first step is the collection of floral nectar from the gullets of colorful and usually fragrant blossoms. Floral nectar starts out as sugar water enriched with a few amino acids, proteins, lipids, phenolics, and other chemicals. While it sits in floral crevices or droplets, waiting to be sampled by pollinators, the nectar takes on the combined aroma of the flowers that secreted it. Though the scent of the nectar itself is faint, the aromas are intensified once it is concentrated into honey. Excess water is driven off and the complex volatile oils and other chemicals from the flower are magnified, becoming part of the honey and adding to its appeal. Single-source honeys reveal their characteristic aromas best at room temperature, especially when drizzled on a warm piece of toast. You can almost smell the flowers. Try some orange blossom or blueberry honey for a real taste treat. Honey that comes from a single kind of flower is most prized by beekeepers and more expensive to buy than blended or mixed-flower honeys.

When a forager returns to the hive, she looks for a nest mate to which she can pass along her precious few microliters of nectar. The younger, stay-at-home honey makers and nurse bees often tap the returning foragers with their antennae, begging for a free taste. The forager and the worker then engage in trophyllaxis, the process by which the forager regurgitates nectar to the "house bee."

*One worker bee is feeding another, her sister. This is called trophyllaxis.*

The faster the worker bee can unload her nectar, the quicker she can be back out in the field foraging for more. The length of time it takes the returning forager to find a willing receiver indicates the status of the honey stores in the colony. If receiver bees are eager to take the nectar, it means the colony is low on honey. If it takes the forager several minutes to find a bee to accept her offering, there is probably plenty of honey already in the combs. Or perhaps the receivers find the quality of the nectar inferior because the sugar level is too low.

When a receiver bee has relieved a forager of her nectar, she transfers it to a waiting cell. Then she stands over the cell and concentrates the nectar, evaporating the excess water by fanning her wings over the liquid and by sucking it back into her mouth and crop, then regurgitating it onto her tongue as many as two hundred times. In this way, she raises the sugar level of the nectar from between 30 and 40 percent to an amazing 80 percent. The higher sugar concentration preserves the honey that she produces, killing microbes by sucking the moisture out of them. If the sugars fall below 80 percent, the honey will lose its ability to withstand degradation by the sugar-loving yeasts. In the United States, honey must be 80 percent sugar to be labeled as honey.

As soon as most of the water has been evaporated, the

*A lone worker bee fans her wings to help control the temperature within the nest.*

bees fan their wings thousands of times over those sections of the comb where the concentrated nectar is stored. This fanning, along with the high temperatures (34 to 36°C) in the nest, helps to thicken and ripen the nectar into honey.

Worker bees constantly check the viscosity of the ripening honey to make sure it achieves just the right consistency. When the honey is fully ripened, other workers cap the storage cells with fresh wax, ensuring that the colony will be well fed over the coming weeks and months.

Or will it? Greedy creatures beyond the hive, coveting what the bees have worked so hard to produce, frequently break into the nest to rob it of its treasure—bears, badgers, skunks, and human honey hunters in the wild, beekeepers and mice when the bees live in managed colonies. Some of the robbed booty will make the long journey from honeycomb to beekeeper to honey jar to breakfast table, assisted by packagers, transporters, and marketers, and finally by sweet-toothed shoppers negotiating crowded supermarket aisles or arriving early morning at a farmers' market to get the freshest possible local honeys.

## Chapter 3
# A Year in the Life of a Beekeeper

TODAY, FEW PEOPLE go into beekeeping with dreams of becoming rich. Although there are some millionaires among the top American honey producers and a few who own tens of thousands of colonies, for most beekeepers it's a matter of passion—quite simply, they love the bees they tend. Call it beecraft.

## The Passion of the Beekeeper

My favorite time of year is the fleeting spring, which arrives in the Sonoran desert around my Tucson home in mid- to late March and has departed by early May. Barely a desert, since it averages twelve inches of rain a year, the Sonoran is home to paloverde trees, shrubs, and annual wildflowers, which in spring paint the washes, hillsides, and creosote bush flats with their magnificent colors—the oranges of Arizona poppies, the cobalt blue of *Phacelia,* the paler blues of lupines, and the pinks and reds of tall-stemmed penstemons and the shorter owl's clover. These flowering plants deck themselves out in such colorful finery to attract prospective sexual go-betweens, the bees, which, as dedicated pollinators, are necessary to the plants' successful reproduction.

Spring always reminds me of when I kept bees. My awakening colonies all teemed with life as their hardworking denizens got down to the various bee tasks. As one group of ten or fifteen bees launched themselves from the landing board, another returned, many of them bearing yellow, orange, and white pollen loads on their broad hind legs. The bees without colorful pollen loads were probably nectar gatherers. About three-quarters of the bees were after nectar, while the remaining fourth foraged for pollen to make into nutritious bee bread. Usually a honey bee worker is either a nectar gatherer or a pollen forager. However, if a nectar gatherer spots a tempting bit of pollen, she may go for it and return to the colony well stocked with both types of food. Over the course of her life, a worker bee will alternate periods of foraging for nectar with periods of specializing in pollen.

To me, the nests seemed like giant pairs of lungs, inhaling the returning foragers, exhaling the departing ones. Hive Breath. That was my favorite way of thinking about my hives—as living organisms breathing out pollinators, who in turn breathe life into the desert plants and the entire ecosystem.

Like most beekeepers in the United States, I kept my charges in those familiar stacked white wooden boxes named Langstroth hives after the man who invented them in the nineteenth century (see page 27 for a detailed description of the Langstroth hive and its history).

The entrances to many of my hives were outfitted with pollen traps, an ingenious if somewhat malevolent device created by curious bee researchers. These traps taught me a lot about the ways of bees and their link to the flowering plants in a foraging domain of roughly five square miles. A pollen trap is made up of closely spaced but slightly askew screens. In order to enter the hive, incoming bees have to run the wire mesh gauntlet, losing about 60 percent of their pollen loads, colorful pellets that fall into a drawer at the bottom of the hive. All I had to do was go around to a hive's back side, open the drawer, and take a sample of pollen. Observing the colors and microscopic characteristics of the grains told me what plants the bees had recently visited. I was able to tell how many kinds of flowers my bees visited, hourly, daily, monthly, or over an entire year. It turned out that on average they visited one-quarter of the floral species blooming within their flight range.

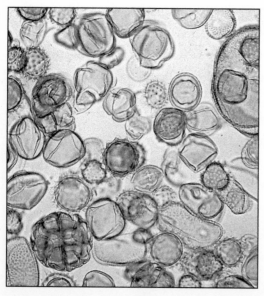

*Typical pollen collected by bees in Arizona magnified by a light microscope.*

Sometimes I took fresh honey from a honey bee nest and studied the pollen grains it contained. For many years, I was like a floral forensics CSI investigator, able to tell what families and genera of plants the bees had visited by spying inside their pantries. The record of trace pollen grains in honey gives a reliable indication of its floral origins. My hives were also placed on platform scales so I knew how much honey the bees had made since I last visited them.

When honey is diluted with water, then spun in a high-speed laboratory centrifuge, the pollen separates out and forms a sediment at the bottom of the centrifuge tube. After some chemical mischief with hot acids and a fume hood, the pollen is transferred to microscope slides. Magnified four hundred times or more, the grains give up their secret identities, for each type of pollen is unique in size, shape, and surface sculpturing. A good palynologist (a scientist who studies pollen) can tell you the family, genus, and sometimes species to which any grain belongs. This is important information for beekeepers, since pure single-source honeys command top dollar, making it necessary to know what kind of blossoms the honey was made from. By sending a sample to a laboratory and having its pollen content analyzed, beekeepers can find out if their tupelo honey really is from tupelo trees. Some countries require honey dealers to submit their single-source honeys to a certified lab for quality control.

I always enjoyed removing the glistening honeycomb

frames from my hives. As rivulets of honey trickled down the face of the comb, they were chased by bees trying to recapture the golden droplets. Ever eager to satisfy my sweet tooth, I would thrust a finger into the comb and lick it clean. Honey is at its best right out of the comb, still warm, and fresh and delicious in a way that is hard to imagine unless you've actually experienced it.

One of the pleasures of beekeeping is the wonderful fragrance of a bees' nest. Once you've inhaled that aroma, it's something you'll never forget. Open a hive on a hot day, remove the cover with your hive tool, and take a deep breath. The essence of the inner nest and its bee inhabitants is in that smell.

But the hive odor is difficult to place. Sometimes it reminds me of a yeasty brewery or winery, sometimes a bakery filled with fresh pastries, especially if some of the combs are uncapped. During my beekeeping years, I was instinctively drawn to the sisterhood of the hive and never tired of peeking inside to see what my bees were doing.

I don't, however, like getting stung. To me, getting stung when working with bees means you are moving too fast, being careless, and crushing bees unnecessarily. A crushed bee gives off a banana-like scent from her special sting glands, an olfactory alarm that triggers a stinging chain reaction among her sisters. As a result, the bees can "go nuclear" on you, trying to plant their barbs in your skin and willing to sacrifice their lives to defend the sanctity of the nest, their home.

# From Hollow Logs to Man-Made Hives:
## The Story of the Reverend L. L. Langstroth,
## the Langstroth Hive, and the Discovery of Bee Space

MANY OF US have seen apiaries, those collections of man-made hives arranged in neat rows along country roads adjacent to blooming crops. But unless you are a beekeeper, you aren't likely to know how one man, the inventor of those boxes, changed the face not just of American beekeeping, but of beekeeping everywhere.

Lorenzo Lorraine Langstroth was a keen observer of honey bee behavior. An ordained minister, he remained a devout clergyman throughout his life. But he was equally devoted to his nonhuman flock—those winged six-legged creatures that live in special housing of his design. Named after the inspired reverend, Langstroth hives are now used around the world by commercial and hobbyist beekeepers alike. For this reason, Langstroth is often regarded as both the father of modern beekeeping and the Henry Ford of hive technology.

Langstroth's insight about "bee space" revolutionized beekeeping. Bee space—or the distance between combs, about $\frac{1}{4}$ to $\frac{5}{16}$ inch—is the amount of wiggle room that bees need as they move around the dark confines of the nest. Bee space is the same whether it's in a man-made Langstroth hive or a nest of the bees' own construction in the wild.

In pre-Langstroth hives, there were no built-in supports for the bees' honeycombs. As a result, the bees built their combs wherever they pleased, and chaos and confusion reigned. Lanstroth recognized that if he provided the bees with wooden frames on which they could build their combs, and if he placed the frames at sufficient distance from each other to create ample maneuvering room, or bee space, the colony would develop in an orderly manner and thrive. Now, for the first time in history, bees were truly being managed. They could be made to build their combs where their keepers wanted.

Although the Langstroth hive harkens back to the Civil War, it has withstood the test of time and is used by most beekeepers.

Langstroth hives are typically made of pine boards half an inch thick. Their exterior surfaces are usually painted white to prevent the wood from rotting and to reflect sunlight in order to keep the hive a bit cooler. In early spring, the hive consists of two or three stories, which beekeepers call supers. Each super is a box that contains several removable rectangular wooden frames on which the bees can build their waxen combs. The frames hang vertically from top bars, inner rims along the upper edges of opposite sides of the super.

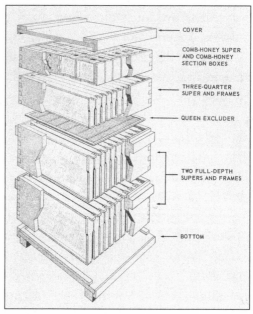

COVER

COMB-HONEY SUPER AND COMB-HONEY SECTION BOXES

THREE-QUARTER SUPER AND FRAMES

QUEEN EXCLUDER

TWO FULL-DEPTH SUPERS AND FRAMES

BOTTOM

*Langstroth-style honey bee hive.*

The combs that are used for storing honey are in the shallower, upper supers, while those for raising the young are in the deeper supers below. As the seasons progress, the nest within the hive can grow twelve stories tall as beekeepers keep adding honey-holding supers to the top of the stack. Giving honey bees more storage room is a way to exploit their natural hoarding tendencies. The more room they have, the bigger the honey harvest. The diagram gives us a look at the interior of a Langstroth hive with all its parts labeled. Unless you come from a beekeeping family, the terminology can be confusing. The supers rest on a bottom board that has wooden cleats nailed to its underside to give the hive a stable foundation. Topping the uppermost supers, where the honey is stored, is the hive cover or lid. This keeps out the sun, wind, and rain and provides the bees with a cozy, comfortable home.

Let's examine the lowermost super of the hive, which rests on the bottom board. The bees build combs in the frames of this chamber, which they use as nurseries to rear their brood or as pantries to store the pollen they have made into bee bread. Little or no honey is stored here.

Resting on the bottom one or two supers is a metal grid that looks a bit like a barbeque grate. This is the queen excluder, a simple device that beekeepers use to manage their colonies. Worker bees can easily squeeze through the parallel bars of the excluder, but the larger queen cannot. With an excluder in place, the queen is confined to the nursery below, which means she can't lay her eggs in the upper stories, making it easier for the beekeeper to extract the honey.

The upper supers are generally shallower than the ones below. This is because shallow supers full of stored honey weigh about thirty-eight pounds, easier to lift than the eighty pounds a deep super full of honey weighs. Nevertheless, many a beekeeper complains of a bad back due to a lifetime of lifting and stacking full honey supers.

## The Beekeeper's Bees

While stingless bees have long been established in the Americas, honey bees, native to the Old World, didn't arrive until the sixteenth century, when Spanish settlers imported them, hoping to replace the bees of the Maya with their own, more productive kind. Soon the newcomers were swarming their way north toward what is now the United States, where they joined honey bees introduced in the seventeenth century by English colonists with beekeeping ambitions. Early accounts indicate that these enterprising bees, called "white man's flies" by Native Americans, were colonizing new territory at the rate of at least fifty miles a year. According to records of the period, the advancing honey bee front was often one hundred to two hundred miles ahead of the American frontier.

It was the European honey bee that would eventually populate the Langstroth hives of most of America's modern beekeepers.

## The Beekeeper's Year

Unless you buy your honey from a farmers' market, roadside stand, or beekeeping neighbor, it most likely comes from one of the huge honey marketers such as the Sioux Honey Association, a cooperative association of 375 large-scale beekeeping operations, which produces forty million pounds of honey each year.

The big honey packers and distributors get their honey from beekeepers all over the United States, especially Florida and the Dakotas, bargaining with them to acquire their harvest at the lowest possible price. The largest beekeeping operation in the United States is Adee Honey Farms in Bruce, South Dakota, with over seventy-five thousand hives, a major commercial pollinator of California almond orchards.

Whether the colonies number ten or seventy-five thousand, there is a rhythm to the beekeeper's life. At certain times of the year, different things need to happen in the beeyard, following a natural sequence of events that cannot be ignored or disrupted. These are the seasons of the beekeeper, which vary little, especially if the bees are kept in the temperate United States.

## The Beekeeper's Spring

Spring is the busiest time of year for honey bees and their keepers, whether the operation is in the desert uplands of southern Arizona, the citrus groves of Florida, or the apple orchards of Washington State.

The first wildflowers of spring beckon both the bees and their human landlords. In the far northern states, the bees have been hive-bound for months and are ready to get outside and buzz through the warm, fragrant air. Bees of foraging age act as scouts, the first to venture out into the big world beyond the hive. As soon as they locate the earliest spring blooms, they return to the nest and perform a waggle dance, which communicates the location of the new food sources to their fellow foragers. There may still be some fall honey stored in the hive, but there is probably very little pollen, or bee bread, left in the darkened brood combs, so the bees need to bring in lots of protein- and lipid-rich pollen pellets. The nitrogen and amino acids in the pollen will nourish new bees, which, when mature, will bring in yet more pollen and nectar to feed and fuel the ever-growing colony.

Good beekeepers inspect their colonies regularly during the spring. They know that if a colony is in good health in early spring, it will have stored a surplus of honey by late spring and early summer. (To rent their colonies for crop pollination, a healthy population is essential.) The surplus honey will be harvested and sold at farm stands or to the big packers for distribution across the country and around the world.

Using the bellows of a bee smoker to puff cool, dense white smoke into the hive to quiet its residents, the keeper examines the lowermost super to gauge the condition of the brood, assess the health of the queen, and detect the presence of eggs, disease, or parasitic mites. In the uppermost supers of the hive, the beekeeper looks for evidence of new honey production: Are the bees producing fresh wax to construct extra storage combs for their spring or summer crop?

Spring is the time to treat the bees for diseases such as American or European foulbrood, nosema, or chalkbrood. Healthy bees and a rapidly growing population are necessary for the colony to produce enough foragers to bring home the nectar and pollen. A weakened or sick colony is a drain on the beekeeper's time and finances. Weak colonies often require supplemental feeding with a sugar solution or corn syrup to grow rapidly and become strong enough to earn their keep. Sometimes a beekeeper will construct a sugar-water feeder out among the colonies. There is the danger, however, that this open source of free sugar will incite a feeding frenzy, causing the bees to rob neighboring colonies to satisfy their craving for more carbohydrates. The bees can become defensive during a feeding frenzy, and beekeepers, friends, and neighbors are likely to be stung.

Spring, of course, also means spring cleaning—and the hives are in serious need of it. Mice may have entered some of the colonies in the fall and caused damage to the combs. These combs, as well as any damaged by tunneling wax moth larvae, are removed by the beekeeper and replaced with fresh or recycled frames. To allow the colonies to grow, the beekeeper may add an extra brood super holding eight to ten deep frames. Up in the honey attic, one or more shallow supers may be added to make room for the expected production.

### THE BEEKEEPER'S SUMMER

*A swarm of bees in May*
*Is worth a cow and bottle of hay*
*A swarm of bees in July*
*Is not worth a fly.*
　　　—"A Reformed Commonwealth of Bees," 1655

For most beekeepers, no matter where they live in the continental United States, summer, like spring, is a busy time of year. There's always something to do in the beeyard. What with harvesting honey, installing new supers, painting hives, fixing old bee trucks, and repairing honey house equipment, there aren't many moments when beekeepers can sit by idly and just enjoy their bees.

Collecting the nectar when the flow is on is the name of the beekeeping game. Although nectar flows can occur in the spring and even into the fall, bees stockpile their largest surpluses during the summer months. This is also the time of the year when honey bee populations are at their peak. Sixty thousand bees living in one hive isn't uncommon.

During the summer, the bees work from dawn to dusk, each bee of foraging age making five, eight, or even twelve trips a day several miles from the nest. Sunshine is plentiful, grasses shimmer in the warm breezes, and flowers abound. This is a great time to be alive if you're a honey bee—or a beekeeper.

When the bees work from dawn to dusk, so do their keepers. If the nectar is coming in fast (averaging three to five pounds per colony per day), the beekeeper must work hard assembling extra honey supers from parts previously ordered. As soon as the old supers are full, the beekeeper removes and replaces them with the new ones, ready to take on more liquid gold. The secret of good beekeeping is knowing when the nectar flow is on and then gently managing the colonies by adding or removing supers and frames as required. A scale colony (literally a hive upon a scale) in an apiary is the very best way to know what the bees have been up to. Summer nectar flows are the prime flows in almost all parts of the country. In Arizona, this is when the velvet mesquite produces a second flush of blooms full of nectar and the hum of bees. Around Tucson, summer is the season when our state flower, the saguaro cactus, puts out its massive white blooms. The morning after the cactuses bloom, honey bees head for the nectar- and pollen-rich saguaro flowers, competing with native cactus bees, flickers, woodpeckers, and white-winged doves for the tasty treats. We also get good summer nectar flows from acacias, especially if the monsoon rains heading north out of Mexico reach us during July and the plants respond by flowering early.

The summer nectar flow peaks at different times in various regions of the country. Some flows are brief, lasting but a day or a week at most. Other flows might go on for a month.

For the nation's thousand or so migratory beekeepers, summer's blooms are the signal to hit the road with their eighteen-wheelers packed with hives. Few people know about these relatively small-scale operations, which roll down the interstates, following the nectar flow for thousands of miles. When the mobile beekeepers find a promising spot, near an apple orchard or citrus grove, they unload their hives with small forklifts, and gently place them near the blooms so the gathering of nectar can begin. The goal is to harvest a lot of honey, especially high-value, single-source honeys such as those from white clover and aromatic orange blossoms.

Many migratory beekeepers also derive a large portion

of their income from pollination hive rental fees paid by farmers and orchard owners, eager to ensure that their fields and groves will be well pollinated in order to bear the highest-quality fruit.

Late summer is the time to collect honey produced during the nectar flows earlier in the season. Small-time beekeepers generally do their honey processing in their kitchens or garages. But large-scale commercial beekeepers load the honey-heavy supers from the hives onto a truck and transport them to a honey house, where the crop will be harvested.

You can usually locate the honey house in an apiary because it is bombarded with hundreds of bees buzzing excitedly around the building in a determined, if futile, effort to break in for a quick meal.

## The Beekeeper's Autumn

As summer advances into fall, there is a crisp chill in the air that migratory birds and honey bees notice long before the first frost warnings appear in the local newspapers. And as the season changes, so do the colors of the floral landscape. Pinks, blues, and lavenders give way to the warm yellows of the sunflower family. Asters, coneflowers, and goldenrod abound, spreading across meadows and bordering country roads and forest paths. This is the last big bloom of the year, and the pollinators know it. Honey bees, bumble bees, leafcutter bees, and sweat bees all jostle one another on crowded blossoms, scrambling to harvest the last of the season's nectar and pollen.

The race is on, for the winter ahead will be long and arduous, and it is critical, for honey bees, at least, to store enough sugar in the form of honey to wait out the cold. There will be no flowers on the horizon or excursions out of the hive until the seasons turn and spring comes around once again. But there may be sufficient honey produced during this season to give the beekeeper one last harvest, while still leaving enough to get the bees through the coming months.

Beekeepers in autumn are just as busy as their bees. They must be especially vigilant, for though fall swarming isn't common, it does happen. Loss of half the population of a hive in the fall means the colony will probably die out over the winter. To prevent the bees' swarming to a new hive, the beekeeper needs to add an empty super to the hive, filled with ten frames of beeswax foundation, so the colony has room to grow and the bees don't feel pressed to find a new home. Sheets of man-made, hexagonally stamped foundation consisting of pure beeswax, sometimes coated in plastic, are purchased from a bee supply house and give the bees a head start in their construction efforts. Fall is also the time to combine two weak colonies into one strong one that is sure to last the winter and be ready for the spring nectar flow.

When fall comes, many beekeepers install entrance reducers in the narrow, mouthlike colony doorways. An entrance reducer is a thin piece of wood cut to the width and length of the entrance, with a notch in the middle to allow the bees to come and go. It fits snugly into the entrance opening and can be tightly secured with a nail or two. Entrance reducers keep winter drafts out of the colony and make it easier to prevent the invasion of field mice and other predators. Seeking the warmth and rich store of food found in the hive during the winter months, the mice can be very destructive to bee colonies. Although the bees eventually sting them to death and entomb them behind walls of resinous bee glue called propolis, they can wreak havoc before being dispatched to their untimely end. (Embalmed mouse mummies are an interesting side note to beekeeping.)

Autumn is a time of great floral abundance. If the colonies are located near a big meadow of goldenrod and asters, the bees may produce quite a haul. (Honey from asters is not everyone's favorite—many even consider it downright rank. But to me it's full-bodied and flavorful, capturing the true essence of the season.) Beekeepers who harvest honey in the fall must not be greedy, for if they take too much, the colony will run through its reserves before winter has ended and another round of nectar collecting and honey making can begin.

Fall is a good time to inspect your bee colonies. Are the bee populations strong and healthy, free of foulbrood, nosema, or chalkbrood? Has dry rot attacked the wooden hives, requiring new parts? Some beekeepers move their hives to sheltered spots out of the wind and protected from the cold. Winter is coming—the bees know it, and the beekeepers make ready.

# The Beekeeper's Winter

Winter, not surprisingly, is the time for "wintering" the hives to protect them from the change in weather, at least in northern states. When actively keeping bees, I was fortunate not to have to do any wintering, other than making sure my colonies had adequate honey stores. For beekeepers at higher elevations or in the Northeast, it's an entirely different story. There, winter blizzards and intense cold pose a serious health risk for the bees. The thin pine lumber used in most man-made hives doesn't offer enough protection from the howling winds of a nor'easter. In these areas, the more thermal protection a colony gets, the less honey the hunkered-down bees need to keep their internal fires stoked and their cellular machinery going. For cold-weather beekeepers, wintering hives often involves wrapping the entire colony with insulating materials such as straw, plastic, or even Styrofoam.

Another threat during the winter months are the blankets of snow that can completely bury a colony. When this happens, the beekeeper must clear the hive entrances so the bees inside won't suffocate.

Throughout the long, cold months, the bees congregate in what is called the winter cluster, a tight sphere of bee bodies forty thousand strong, usually located near their stored cache of honey. They are literally huddling to keep warm. It's called thermoregulation, and the bees are experts at it. By eating honey, then shivering their flight muscles without moving their wings, they can raise their internal body temperatures significantly. Revving their mini-engines keeps not only individual bees warm, but their neighbors as well. The temperature will not dip below 68°F within the cluster. When bees in the outermost layers start feeling chilly, they push their way deep into the core, the warmest part of the cluster. Wouldn't you?

With their clustering ways and furry coats, the bees can survive freezing or even subfreezing weather. They do pay a price, however, because all those burned calories must come from their stored honey. If the beekeeper has taken too much honey in the fall, it could mean disaster in the months that follow.

Winter is a good time for the beekeeper to work indoors, studying beecraft by reading *The ABC and XYZ of Bee Culture* or going through back issues of *American Bee Journal* that there was no time for during the busier seasons of the year. Newbie beekeepers might use the downtime to assemble more frames or to repair damaged supers, hive lids, and bottom boards. A forward-thinking beekeeper might go online and look for the latest in disease-resistant queens and package bees from bee breeders in Hawaii, New Zealand, or Georgia.

Despite the cold winds that blow regularly across the apiaries, there are usually a few warm days when temperatures rise above 55°F and the bees can escape their winter clusters and venture outside. There are no flowers to tempt them, but necessity calls. The problem with clustering is that the bees don't have an opportunity to relieve themselves. The adult bees are hygienic creatures and will not foul their nests with their own excrement;

they need to fly out of the hive to take care of important business. Beekeepers euphemistically refer to these winter breaks as "cleansing flights."

And now it's time for yet another change in season. As a result of all the beekeeper's cold-weather chores, the colonies come out of the winter months healthy, well fed, and ready to gorge on the abundant nectar and pollen of spring.

## And Here Comes the Swarm

Swarming, a natural event in the biology of honey bees, is their way of increasing their numbers. It can happen anytime during the year, depending on the race of bee, the weather, and the flowering calendar in the area where the bees live. European honey bees, for example, usually swarm once or twice during the late spring, while the Africanized bees (the so-called "killer bees") in southern Arizona swarm many times throughout the year.

The bees know when their colony has become overpopulated, whether it's established in the cozy hollow of a stately tree or in a manufactured wooden hive. Overcrowding is the signal to head out and start a new colony with room to grow and expand.

Prior to the actual swarming event, scout bees venture out on reconnaissance flights and inspect every hollow tree, rock outcropping, and large cavity in the neighborhood. Is it dry inside, protected from the elements, and near plenty of flowering plants? Are neighboring (and competing) bee colonies too close to the parental nest?

Eventually, dozens or even hundreds of scouts converge

on the new location. Somehow a consensus has been reached and group action takes hold. Now it's time to begin the move. Returning to the hive, the scouts perform waggle dances, thought to inform the other bees of the location of their new home.

Meanwhile, the scouts that have remained at the new home site to stake their claim form a circle around the entrance, facing outward. Assuming a characteristic tail-up, head-down stance, each bee fans its wings into a blur as it exposes the glistening Nasanov gland near the tip of the abdomen. The gland secretes a flowery potpourri of chemicals that will help the migrants find their way to the new residence.

As the swarming process begins, thousands of bees pour out of the old colony and settle on the ground. Thousands more clamber up the walls of the hive in dark festoons. Many take to the air and swirl in looping flights around the soon-to-be-abandoned nest. Eventually, the old queen, a few hundred drones (male bees), and usually half of the nest's workers (sterile females) are hovering in the air, ready to move to the new location. There are no real leaders, but somehow the system works and the swarm takes off, slowly at first, then faster, a giant, seething mass moving through the spring morning like an ominous storm cloud. The swarm may contain twenty thousand bees or more and can be one hundred feet wide and twenty to thirty feet tall.

I've been lucky as a bee researcher and part-time bee-keeper to witness the swarming spectacle dozens of times. I've even experienced the adrenaline rush of running inside several swarms as they moved to their new lodgings. It's called swarm running, and I do it just for fun. The bees are gentle, their stomachs full of honey for the trip, and they are not in the mood to sting. As I run, bees swirl about me in all directions, but somehow the mass stays together, changing shape but not dispersing. As the swarm pulses its way forward, it ramps up to top "bee speed," 15 mph on the wing. Though a former long-distance runner, I have to struggle to keep up, and the swarm inevitably leaves me in the dust, my heart pounding as I gasp for breath and wonder where the bees will finally settle in.

Although I find running with the bees an exhilarating experience, to beekeepers, swarms are nothing but trouble. When bees leave an apiary, they are usually gone for good. Each colony that produces a swarm loses half its bees and therefore half its honey-making potential. To prevent swarming and increase their colonies, many beekeepers make "divides." After selecting a large, populous hive, the beekeeper turns it into two hives by dividing the supers and placing them on two separate stands, each with bottom boards and a cover. At least one or two frames of emerging or capped brood cells are placed in the lower supers, along with three or four frames covered with worker bees. Usually, no effort is made to locate the original queen. The beekeeper leaves it to Mother Nature and the colony to produce an unmated queen in the queenless half of the artificially divided colony.

# Chapter 4
# Staying in Touch:
# The Beekeeper's Craft

WHILE HONEY HUNTING provides adventure and a connection to age-old traditions, beekeeping is a lot easier and more practical, and it has a long history as well. The keeping of bees is but one aspect of the strong human urge to conquer the natural world. We've tamed wild dogs and cats, cattle, and horses, turning them into obedient pets, docile milk producers, and sturdy mounts. We've rerouted rivers, plowed under ancient forests, drained swamps and reinvented these once-wild places as gated communities and golf courses. So it's hardly surprising that we manage bees, bending them to our will, channeling their natural honey-making instincts to our own purposes, whether it is to satisfy our urge for sticky buns or to create healing unguents and preservatives.

Beekeepers are not average citizens. It's their passion for bees that sets them apart. Most people in Western countries, especially the United States, have pronounced entomophobia, a fear of insects. A tiny creature buzzing around the head seems to send most normal folks packing, or at least reaching for a can of bug spray.

Not so with beekeepers, for they have an intuitive understanding of their bees, can sense their "moods," predict their actions, and anticipate their every need. They have even developed unique ways of communicating with their fuzzy, honey-producing charges—a private language of words, sounds, and song. There is an almost magical quality that binds beekeepers and bees.

But when did this strange passion called beekeeping begin? About seven thousand years ago, the trend toward a sedentary life changed the relationship between humans and honey bees. In addition to robbing their nests in the wild, we began raising them on our farms and in the backyards of houses in our villages.

The first beekeepers may have simply chopped out inhabited sections of bee trees and carried the boles back to their settlements to protect them from the ravages of other honey-loving predators. Centuries later, the Aryan Indians and the Egyptians refined the process.

Beekeeping in India can be traced back four thousand years. Honey was used not only as a cooking ingredient in Vedic India, but also as a medicine with wide-ranging therapeutic applications. It also played a significant role in Vedic myths and religious rituals. During marriage ceremonies, for example, the bride's body was anointed with honey to ensure fertility. And after the ceremony was over, honey was served to the guests because it was believed that a substance so pure would ward off any evil spirits that might try to crash the festivities. With honey on the menu and evil spirits kept at bay, the newlyweds could expect to have a happy, fruitful, and prosperous married life.

Vedic beekeepers housed their honey makers in hives constructed of twigs and grasses covered in dried mud, as well as in clay pots. The hives were typically kept in wall niches or hung from the ceiling in farmyard outbuildings. As is the case in many parts of the world, both historically and in the present day, Indian beekeepers used smoke to pacify their bees while they helped themselves to their honey. They were, however, wise enough to leave sufficient honey in the hive to ensure that the bees remained well fed and productive. Overpopulated colonies were often divided to create new ones—still a common practice among beekeepers around the world. Empty hives were sometimes hung from trees in the forest and smeared with beeswax and sweet palm sap to encourage swarming bees to settle in. Once the bees had established themselves in their new home, the beekeeper would bring the now populated hive back to the farmyard so that the honey could be conveniently harvested.

Lower Egypt, well watered and fertilized by the annual flooding of the Nile, seems to have been the center of organized beekeeping in the ancient world. In fact, bees and honey were so important to the economy of Lower Egypt that the honey bee hieroglyph was chosen as the symbol of the entire region.

*An incised Egyptian tomb hieroglyph of a bee, the symbol of royalty. From a door lintel, King Intef.*

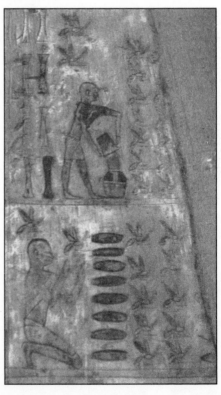

*Ancient Egyptian beekeeper pouring honey into a container. Incised and painted relief on a stone pillar in the tomb of Pabesa, West Bank, Upper Egypt, 664–625 BC.*

Honey wasn't the only reason to raise bees. Always practical, the Egyptians put beeswax to good use in a number of ways, including mummification, shipbuilding, the lost-wax casting of sacred objects in precious metals, and as a kind of gel to keep their elaborate high-fashion wigs slicked down and firmly in place!

Egyptian beekeeping practices influenced successful bee management throughout the Mediterranean world. We know that the Greeks and Romans were avid bee-keepers and consumed honey in great quantities. In fact, the Romans elevated beekeeping to a fine art—so fine that the great Roman poet Virgil wrote about it in lyric verse. In book four of the *Georgics*, his famous treatise on agriculture and beekeeping, Virgil covered just about everything a beekeeper needed to know, from the ideal location of the apiary to the social value of bees as role models . . .

*Let there be clear springs nearby, and pools green with moss, and a little stream sliding through the grass.*

. . . to its proper maintenance . . .

*You keep them warm too, with clay smoothed by your fingers round their cracked hives, and a few leaves on top.*

. . . to how to control a swarm of bees on the wing . . .

49

*Scatter . . . balm and corn parsley's humble herb and
make
A tinkling sound [with cymbals]:
They'll settle themselves on the soporific rest sites:
They'll bury themselves, as they do, in their deepest
cradle.*

Virgil also praised the communal values of honey bee
society:

*They alone hold children in common: own the roofs
of their city as one: and pass their life under the might
of the law.
They alone know a country, and a settled home,
and in summer, remembering the winter to come,
undergo labour, storing their gains for all.*

Virgil's glimpses into life in the hive advanced the notion of bee society as a model that human society would
do well to emulate.

Organized beekeeping, which had thrived and spread
throughout the entire Roman Empire, went into a decline after the demise of the Pax Romana, which lasted
for about 207 years. During the Dark Ages in Europe (AD
500 to 1000), and especially after the ruinous invasions
of the eastern hordes, apiculture nearly ceased in many
parts of the continent. Most people had to make do with
hunting honey in the forests. Toward the end of the Dark
Ages, Charlemagne, the first Holy Roman Emperor (AD

800 to 814), laid down rules governing any beekeeping that was still practiced—rules having mostly to do with taxation to fill the royal treasury. Beekeepers were obliged to pay the emperor dues in kind: two-thirds of all their honey and one-third of their beeswax. After Charlemagne died, *abeillage,* or "bee dues," remained a feudal right. Every vassal owed the sovereign a generous portion of what the hives produced.

Even before their colonization by Rome during the reign of Emperor Claudius (10 BC to AD 54), the ancient Britons were so famous for their beekeeping skills that the seafaring Phoenicians, who regularly visited the island on trading expeditions, referred to it as the "Isle of Honey," as did local Druid bards. Under Roman rule, the country produced and consumed vast quantities of honey, both as a sweetener and in the form of mead, the honey wine that was their beverage of choice in the days before neighborhood pubs. Centuries later, at the end of the Dark Ages, the Domesday Book, a record of the great survey of England that was completed in 1086 for William the Conqueror, mentions that a goodly number of managed beehives could still be found throughout the kingdom. After milling, fishing, and mining, beekeeping was the most prevalent industry in the land. Unlike their Continental counterparts, English beekeepers apparently prospered throughout the Dark Ages.

During the period AD 1000 to 1300, apiculture, the tending of honey bees, was a common practice at monasteries across the Continent. Hives were built into special niches in cloister walls or placed in bee gardens, where they were tended more or less in the wild.

*Straw skeps and a beekeeper. Woodcut engraving from Sebastian Munster's Cosmographia (Bern, 1545).*

The bees were generally kept in "skep hives" woven from straw coils, with round conical tops smeared with cow dung as waterproofing. Skep hives were much lighter and easier to manage than the clumsy, heavy log hives that they replaced. They were also inexpensive to make and could be expanded as the colony grew by adding more straw coils, called ekes, to the bottom (hence the expression "to eke out"). The downside of straw hives was that they sometimes went up in flames when their owners suspended them over fire pits to pacify the bees with smoke.

Not only did skep hives provide housing for bees throughout Europe at this time, they were also the symbols adopted by the beekeeper and candlemaker guilds and appeared on signs over candle shops to advertise their wares. The skep hive is still considered the symbol of beekeeping, is the state symbol of Utah, and can be found imprinted on modern ceramic honey pots for use on the dining table.

## Forest Beekeeping

The notion of keeping bees in their original forest nests, from which beekeepers could harvest honey and beeswax at will, may have begun as an intermediate stage between honey hunting and true beekeeping in apiaries. There is archaeological evidence that forest beekeeping was practiced two thousand years ago in the heavily wooded areas of northern Europe, but we mainly know about it from the charming woodcut prints in medieval manuscripts depicting forest beekeeping scenes.

Forest beekeeping was especially common in medieval Russia. The forests, most of which were owned by princes, other aristocrats, and monasteries, were worked by beekeepers known as *bortniks* (*bort* means "hollow tree trunk"), who paid sizable rents to their landlords. Bortniks cut distinguishing marks into the bark of bee trees to stake their claim to the residents and the honey they produced. In the eleventh and twelfth centuries, laws were passed to safeguard the bees by imposing heavy penalties on anyone found destroying a bee tree.

When forest beekeepers claimed a wild nest, they often enlarged the tree cavity and expanded the entrance in the front of the nest to make harvesting easier. If the nest was located high in a tree, the beekeepers cut footholds into the trunk for climbing. Forest beekeepers also used climbing ropes and ladders to gain access to the treasure contained in the tree hollow. To discourage competition from honey-hungry bears, the beekeepers sometimes hammered sharp spikes into the tree trunk. Forest beekeeping was also practiced in medieval Germany and Eastern Europe. In England, you can still see remains of the earthen embankments and stone walls that protected medieval bee gardens from the ravages of wild pigs, badgers, and other rapacious honey hunters.

## Stingless Bees and Their Devoted Mayan Keepers

Among the world's beekeepers, none surpassed the pre-Columbian Maya in their devotion to their furry honey-making captives. The ancient Maya, who inhabited the region of what is today southern Mexico, lowland Guatemala, and central Belize, developed colorful rituals to define and celebrate their complex relationship with their bees. Over the course of many centuries, these elaborate rituals became one of the cornerstones of their remarkably enduring culture.

The husbandry of stingless bees (*Melipona* and less

frequently *Trigona*) among the Maya dates back at least one thousand years. Not only did they cherish their bees—which nested in hollow logs in village gardens—but they depended on the bees' honey for a wide range of uses. It was considered an effective treatment for cataracts, conjunctivitis, and chills and fever. As an offering to the gods, it was believed to sweeten the disposition of even the most bloodthirsty deity. And of course it was a prized food. Honey from stingless bees had (and still has) a complex, distinctive taste, quite different from that produced by the more common European honey bee. Honey was also an important item of trade for the Maya, sent by sea to Honduras and Nicaragua as well as by land throughout Mexico. In exchange for honey and beeswax, the Mayans received cacao seeds and precious stones. Stingless bees were not only a critical source of medicine, food, and trade for the Maya, but were also essential to their agriculture, for the prodigious bees pollinated no fewer than sixteen crops grown in the region. Early on, Mayan farmers recognized the importance of stingless bees as pollinators and kept them in colonies near their raised dooryard kitchen gardens. They also formed beeswax into models for the lost-wax casting of gold jewelry and religious objects.

We don't know exactly how the Maya became beekeepers. Perhaps in the early stages of their culture, when they were still hunter-gatherers, they witnessed giant anteaters and other mammals stealing honey from bee nests in hollow tree cavities and realized that helping themselves to the sweet treasure inside would be easier if they first chopped the tree down. And having cut down the trees, they may then have brought the sections where the bees nested back to their villages—a practice that would have led directly to beekeeping.

*A Mayan deity raises a log hive* (jobone) *of their sacred bee,* Melipona beecheii, *the prized honey producer of the Yucatán Peninsula. A stylized bee hovers nearby. From the ancient Mayan screenfold book, the Madrid Codex.*

Although much of this is speculative, we do know that the Maya kept their bees in hollowed logs called *jobones,* each of which contained a nest that was two to four feet long. The logs were stacked on an A-frame rack that was kept in the shade of a palm-thatched, palapa-like hut called the *nahil-kab,* or bee house. An entrance hole, often marked with a cross, was made in the middle of the log. Both ends were sealed with wood or stone discs to keep out army ants and other predators. The beekeepers could simply remove an end plug and reach inside to harvest the honey. Many of these stone discs, elaborately carved with Mayan glyphs, have been recovered by archaeologists throughout the region.

Mayan beekeeping practices adhered strictly to traditions established in prehistoric times and recorded later in a thousand-year-old document called the Madrid Codex, found in the Yucatán by eighteenth-century Spanish explorers (its exact provenance remains unknown). The sacred text made it clear that the fates of bees and their human keepers were inextricably intertwined. When, for example, a beekeeper died, his heir had to inform the bees of the sad news while reassuring them that they would still be well cared for. The new beekeeper could not participate in any of the death rites lest his sadness disturb the sensitive bees. Should he visit a cemetery, the beekeeper could not interact with his bees for at least three weeks or serious harm would come to them. No Mayan would ever have asked a beekeeper to help lay out the corpse of a departed family member or friend, for if a beekeeper touched a dead body, he had to wash his hands and arms several times a day for three weeks with the leaves of an orange tree. He had to perform these cleansing rituals thoroughly before daring to approach his hives. If a bee was accidentally killed, it had to be carefully folded in a leaf and solemnly buried.

Carrying out these rituals was an intrinsic part of the Mayan beekeeper's life. If the rituals were not honored, the bees could become unproductive. Another form of insurance against failing productivity was the beekeeper's constant dialogue with his bees. Staying in touch with the bees helped keep their special relationship going.

Numerous findings from archaeological sites help document the reverence the Maya felt not only for their stingless bees but also for Ah-Mucen-Cab, the god of beekeeping, bees, and honey. The Madrid Codex clearly directs beekeepers to honor the god with festivities to ensure a good flow of honey in the coming season.

## Chapter 5

# The Beginning of an Enduring Passion: Prehistoric Honey Hunters

FROM PREHISTORIC TIMES to the present, we humans have felt a mysterious and enduring connection to these fascinating insects and the food they produce. People have endowed bees with magical properties, attributed to them surprising healing and cleansing powers, and seen in them meaningful symbols representing some of our most profoundly held beliefs.

Our fascination with bees is deeply rooted in our collective consciousness. We see it in the cave paintings that our prehistoric ancestors left behind. We can read it in the rich, complex rituals and traditions that evolved to govern our relationship with these admirable insects. And we can still catch the reverberations of our instinctive connection to that part of the natural world every time a husband calls his wife "honey" or an excited child chases a buzzing bee through a bright summer afternoon. But its influence is much more far-reaching than you might imagine, extending not just to everyday moments of affection and play but to diverse cultures, religious beliefs, cuisines, and scientific study around the world. We can look for its roots in our history and, before that, our prehistory.

Thanks to petroglyphs (rock art), the spectacular painted records still visible on cave walls throughout Europe, Africa, Asia, and even Australia, we know our ancestors definitely had a sweet tooth, and we know that they indulged it by embarking on strenuous and often dangerous honey hunts, armed with tools that enabled them to pillage bee nests with remarkable efficiency. We don't know why cave artists put so much effort into recording these often dramatic hunts. Perhaps the honey hunts signified something more profound than the simple harvesting of an ingredient to sweeten their days, something with deep religious or ceremonial meaning. Whatever the reason, vivid paintings chronicling those honey-hunting expeditions—beautifully stylized yet powerfully real—have been found on the ceilings and walls of hundreds of caves spanning the globe.

Did the rituals of the hunt serve to enlighten them or to give them spiritual guidance? Did they inspire these nomadic clans to strive for the same kind of efficient, productive social organization that the bees had so wonderfully evolved? And what role did honey play in their daily lives? Was it a key ingredient in their primitive cuisine, a medicine used to cure a number of ills, or simply eaten raw as a palate-pleasing, energy-supplying snack after a long day of hunting or gathering foods?

Despite the dedicated work of many archaeologists, we'll probably never know the answers to these questions.

But based on hunting scenes found in caves separated by thousands of miles (and executed with uncanny similarity), we can safely say that raiding bee nests has been an important human activity for millennia, all over the globe. In fact, there are places in the world today where the ancient rituals of those long-ago honey hunters are still practiced virtually unchanged. In the rain forests of Malaysia, the remote valleys of Nepal, and the vast Australian outback, honey-hunting clans set out on expeditions so similar to those depicted in prehistoric cave art that those paintings might well have served as their primers. Let's travel back in time, to a cave that contains one of the most vivid of the ancient honey-hunting paintings.

Like nearly everything our ancestors used, honey had to be collected from the natural world around them—right from the nests of the bees themselves. Except for a small number of tropical wasps and ants, no other creatures collect and store concentrated reserves of sugar the way honey bees, stingless bees, and bumble bees do.

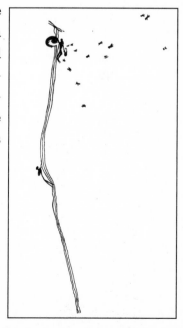

*Petroglyph showing honey collection from a wild bee hive. Cave of the Spider, Valencia, Spain.*

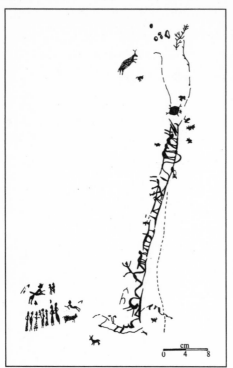

*Petroglyph depicting honey hunters climbing a tall ladder to plunder a nest. Barranc Fondo, Castellón province, Spain.*

*A solitary African honey hunter from the San culture approaches a wild bee nest amidst flying guard bees. Eland Cave, Drakensberg, KwaZulu Natal, South Africa.*

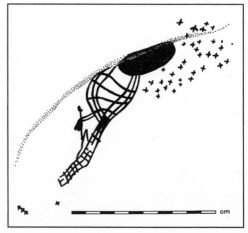

The cave paintings leave no doubt that honey hunting has been going on for thousands of years. Long before the first humans descended from the thorny acacia trees of the African savannas and began a new life as toolmaking, upright bipedal primates, Malaysian honey bears, honey guide birds, and South African honey badgers were all exploiting bee nests. But it was the ingenuity of our early ancestors that turned the honey hunt into a highly ritualized, and effective, activity. It probably didn't take long for prehistoric hunters and gatherers to discover that the nests of certain highly social bees—bumble bees (*Bombus*), stingless bees (*Melipona* and *Trigona*), and honey bees (*Apis mellifera* and other species in the genus *Apis*)—contained plentiful honey. And once they had figured that out, it was doubtless a short step to learning how to attack and exploit these tasty, energy-rich bee nests.

No one has been able to trace the evolution of the human sweet tooth, which is certainly at the root of our passion for bees and honey. We do know that our ape and chimpanzee relatives have a well-developed taste for sugar and aren't shy about availing themselves of any opportunity to gorge on it. And we also know that besides the honey from bees, the only other concentrated sources of sugar available to early humans would have been fruits, berries, and certain tropical grasses. So the honey stored by bees was a prize well worth enduring the stings delivered by the guardians of the nests. Other "spoils of war" from the nests included the juicy, protein-rich brood, consisting of bee larvae and pupae, along with equally nutritious pollen. It is little wonder that so many kinds of mammals and birds in the prehistoric world developed a taste for honey and young bees, along with the necessary skills for locating bee nests and breaking into their well-stocked larders.

Graphic depictions of honey hunting can be found at numerous sites throughout Africa. In fact, Africa has more petroglyphs and associated honey-hunter sites than any other continent. Paintings showing bees, hunters, and the ladders, torches, and honey containers necessary to carry out the raids have been found on rock walls from Algeria, Libya, and Morocco in northern Africa to Namibia, Botswana, and Zimbabwe in the south. Much of this art communicates a sense of the respect, even awe, that our ancestors must have felt for the bees they robbed. Honeycombs are often depicted in great detail in the rock paintings.

When we look at ancient petroglyphs of bees and honey hunts, we can't help feeling that they are more than mere factual chronicles. Some of the depictions seem to have a true spiritual quality, conveying the sense of a special relationship between the human hunters and the bees they preyed upon. But the precise meaning of what the artists were attempting to communicate has been lost to us. All we can do is speculate, and use our imaginations to try to fill in the blanks.

# Chapter 6

# A Taste of Honey: Sampling Varieties from Around the World

THERE ARE MANY varieties of honey for you to experience, each with its own color, aroma, and distinctive flavor. This chapter is your guide to the delicious and surprising world of honey. I'll introduce you to popular types of honey in the United States, then look at some unusual honeys from other lands.

## The Color of Honey

The first thing you notice about honey is its color, especially if it's been packed in a glass jar that happens to be sitting on your kitchen counter with sunlight streaming through it. The warm glow beckons you to grab a spoon and dive in. Honey can be as clear as water or as dark as molasses, though usually it's somewhere in between, a sort of amber color.

The U.S. Department of Agriculture (USDA) has established standardized grades of color for honey, from the most desirable, water white, through progressively darkening grades—extra white, white, extra light amber, light amber, and finally dark amber. Although darker honeys are more flavorful than lighter ones, packers and distributors know that most consumers prefer lighter honey. I don't know why this is so. I have always preferred medium to darker honeys over their lighter, less flavorful cousins.

The USDA's color guide is used by beekeepers, packers, and judges to rate honey at state fairs. In international trade, the color of honey is generally specified since it's a more objective measurement than flavor.

But what causes these different shades of color? One suggestion is that a natural chemical in honey known as melanoidin (polymers) reacts with pigments in tiny grains of pollen that have dissolved in the honey. (Melanoidins are responsible for the nice browning that happens in bread crusts). Honey also darkens when it is exposed to the air, which causes oxidation. Sugars, especially fructose, react with the amino acids in honey to produce a kind of carmelization. These chemical reactions all nudge white or light amber honey into the darker grades. Honey also darkens as it ages and over time can become nearly black. If honey is heated too much, other chemicals like HMF (hydroxymethylfurfural; that's quite a mouthful) are formed, giving rise to the dark color and burnt flavors.

## The Scent of Honey

When you open a jar of fresh honey, take a moment to savor its aroma. All honeys, even the white ones, have a distinct, beguiling perfume. To fully experience the scent, warm the jar before you open it. The warmer the jar, the better, for heat releases the odorant molecules locked in the thick, viscous liquid.

The scent of honey comes from the flowers the bees visited during their foraging trips. Floral scents originate in scent-releasing patches, called osmophores, on the flowers' petals. Throughout their long evolutionary history, flowering plants, needing to attract pollinators in order to survive, have become expert chemists, creating exotic perfumes that no bee can resist. Thanks to these scents, the bees get to load up on nectar and pollen, the flowering plants are able to reproduce, and we can experience the exquisite aroma of honey.

## The Taste of Honey

The taste of honey depends to some degree on its color. White or extra-light amber honeys have characteristically mild flavors, not as dramatic or bold as some of the darker varieties. Honey from buckwheat flowers, for example, is dark and has an intense flavor I happen to be fond of, though many people find it too strong. Onion honey, which bees produce from onion flowers, is also dark and flavorful but not one of my personal favorites (though it might work on an onion bagel).

If a jar is labeled "wildflower honey," it's likely to be a blend of honeys created from the nectar of many different kinds of flowers growing in one area. Or it might be a mix of honeys from many different parts of the world. Honey packers often blend cheap imported honey, usually from

China or Mexico, with more expensive domestic varieties. This blending produces a standardized product, one that is consistent jar after jar, year after year, but is ultimately rather generic. Unfortunately, blending dulls the great taste you can experience with an unblended honey from a single floral source.

All honeys are not the same. You've probably strolled past supermarket shelves or wandered among the stalls of a farmers' market and seen the honey lineup: clover, wildflower, orange blossom, mesquite, tupelo, and many more. These are the true, unblended, single-source honeys called varietals (just as wines from a single type of grape are called varietals). Tupelo honey, for example, should contain honey made only from the nectar of tupelo blossoms. These varietals, or small-batch boutique honeys, generally cost more, but they are well worth the extra expense.

A few gourmet shops are now stocking their shelves with varietals from other countries—really exotic ones such as Tasmanian leatherwood, eucalyptus, and the flavorful manuka medicinal honey from New Zealand. Look for them, ask for them, and experience the incredible taste difference they make.

Of course, the best way to appreciate the true aroma and flavor of honey is to eat it straight from the comb. The experience is like nothing else in the world. But don't despair. Even if you don't have beekeeping friends, all you really need to become a connoisseur is a jar of unblended honey, a spoon, and a warm slice of toast.

The National Honey Board recognizes sixty-four distinct types of honey sold in the United States or exported overseas. Some of these are blends, but most are varietals, derived from one kind of flowering plant or a few related species in the same genus. You could spend years traveling the country, visiting farmers' markets and beekeepers' roadside stands, sampling the sixty-four officially recognized honeys—which include avocado, Brazilian pepper, cat claw, thistle, pumpkin, and sumac honey, to name a few—as well as the scores of local honeys that the board doesn't classify.

Or you could have a honey-tasting party. I'd suggest choosing five or ten honeys that vary greatly in color, aroma, and flavor. To bring out the full bouquet, very gently heat the jars in a double boiler, or microwave them on a low setting for a few seconds. Warming the honey makes it flow freely (ever tried to drag a spoon through a cold jar of honey?) and releases all those luscious scent and flavor molecules, so you and your guests will be able to truly appreciate them.

You might consider making it a guessing game for your guests. Remove the labels from the honey jars (to keep track of which honey is which, write the name on a piece of paper and put it under the jar), then let everyone take a taste and see if they can identify the floral source.

# Honeys from the
# United States
## COMMON U.S. HONEYS

### Clover Honey (*Trifolium repens*)

Dutch clover is considered a weed when it colonizes a manicured front lawn, but when it's grown as fodder, it creates verdant pastures for both cattle and bees. The honey it yields is white, with a very mild, characteristic honey flavor and aroma that make it one of the best-selling varieties in the United States.

### Buckwheat Honey (*Fagopyrum esculentum*)

Buckwheat has been cultivated since the Middle Ages as a honey plant, thanks to its nectar-rich blossoms. In the deserts of the American Southwest, native buckwheat carpets the land and provides rich forage for hungry bees. Buckwheat honey is usually dark and its flavor is so intense that people either love it or hate it. Some actually liken its taste to that of molasses.

### Goldenrod Honey (*Solidago* spp.)

Have you ever seen broad swaths of yellow painted across a brilliant autumn landscape? The flower responsible is goldenrod, which is also the source of a very popular honey. Because goldenrod is usually the last plant to flower before the frosts come, it's an invaluable asset for both bees and their keepers, since it yields the last honey of the season, the one that allows bees to survive the cold months ahead. The taste of goldenrod honey is not unlike that of a refreshing cup of herbal tea brewed from aromatic dried flowers such as chamomile.

### Mesquite Honey (*Prosopis* spp.)

In the hot, dry climates of Arizona, Texas, and New Mexico, various species of mesquite grow in dense thickets called bosques. Beekeepers set up their apiaries near these bosques to ensure that their bees produce plenty of mesquite honey. One of the most popular varieties in the Southwest, it is light in color, with a mild, delicate flavor that I personally find somewhat bland and nondescript.

### Mint Honey (*Mentha* spp.)

The mint family includes peppermint, spearmint, pennyroyal, and curly mint. Honey bees are partial to mint plants because their small blossoms produce an especially sweet nectar. The light-colored honey has a mild flavor reminiscent of crushed spearmint or peppermint leaves and is perfect in iced tea.

### Orange Blossom Honey (*Citrus* spp.)

Opening a jar of this honey immediately transports me back to my high school and early college days in Placentia, Orange County, Southern California. At that time, the early 1970s, the summer's night air was perfumed by thousands of orange trees and millions of orange blossoms. Happily, the honey captures both this incomparably sweet, lingering scent as well as the flavor of the orange blossoms. Orange blossom honey is one of my top ten favorites, and when you try it, it will probably be on your top ten list as well.

### Sunflower Honey (Helianthus annuus and other spp.)

Thousands of acres in the United States are planted with sunflowers, whose oil, when extracted, is widely used in cooking. Their immense "heads" track the sun as it crosses the sky and offer bees a bountiful feast of nectar and bright orange pollen. Sunflower honey has a floral aroma and taste similar to that of goldenrod honey and is light amber.

## RARER U.S. HONEYS

Now that we've sampled the honeys you're most likely to encounter, it's time to visit the backwoods and rural lanes of America in search of rarer specialty honeys, varietals produced in much smaller quantities and not always readily available.

### Avocado Honey (Persea americana)

Not far from my early boyhood home, in the rugged canyons and hills of San Diego County, California, are vast orchards of avocado trees. A native of Mexico and South America, this tree bears numerous small, greenish flowers from which bees harvest nectar. The velvety honey they produce is medium to dark, with a flavor that packs a bit of a bite and has a piquant aftertaste that some people may not find to their liking. Fortunately, it tastes nothing like the oily avocado fruit, nor does it have much of a detectable odor—after all, who would want guacamole honey?

### American Basswood Honey (*Tilia americana*)

Basswood, a member of the linden family, grows in the hardwood forests of the eastern United States. Its pale yellow flowers yield a light-colored, delicately scented honey known for its distinctive bite (probably due to alkaloids contained in the nectar).

### Blueberry Honey (*Vaccinium* spp.)

The first time I tasted fresh blueberry honey from hives located near the wild blueberry barrens of Maine, I couldn't believe how delicious it was. The delicate but distinctive aroma and flavor of ripe blueberries was present in this light amber honey. Usually, flowers and fruit produced by the same plant have different scents, but in this case they're similar, making blueberry honey a special treat.

### Cranberry Honey (*Vaccinium macrocarpon*)

I once spent time recording the foraging behavior of honey bees and bumble bees in and around the cranberry bogs of Wisconsin. It's difficult to find cranberry honey outside of the relatively few cranberry-growing states (Massachusetts, Maine, New Jersey, Wisconsin,

Washington, and Oregon). But if you can, it's well worth the effort. This honey is light amber, and its flavor is similar to that of cranberries but more subtle, having taken on the delicate aroma of the pink cranberry blossoms from which it is derived.

### Pumpkin Honey (*Cucurbita pepo*)

The brilliant orange blossoms of male and female pumpkin flowers can be as big as a human hand and produce great quantities of nectar. But because there are relatively few blossoms per plant, even large, commercial pumpkin patches yield only small amounts of this dark-colored honey. It is typically harvested just once, in late summer or early fall, after the pumpkins have flowered and their fruits have just begun to appear. Its flavor has been described by at least one purveyor as tasting "squashy," reminiscent of the blossoms themselves.

### Tupelo Honey (*Nyssa sylvatica, Nyssa aquatica*)

One of my all-time favorite honeys comes from the tupelo tree, which blooms in April and May. Actually, there are two kinds of tupelo tree, the black gum or sour gum tree and the water tupelo, both of which grow in wet areas of the Southeast, especially along the rivers of northern Florida. In the past, beekeepers used hollowed tupelo logs as hives for their colonies (shades of the Maya). Tupelo honey is much sought after in the southeastern United States. It is golden amber with a greenish tinge and greatly prized for its floral bouquet and the fact that it doesn't granulate. Tupelo honey had a starring role in the movie *Ulee's Gold* as the crop harvested by Ulee, played by actor and Montana rancher Peter Fonda. Mr. Fonda also keeps blue orchard bees (*Osmia lignaria*) to pollinate his apple trees. Fortunately for northern and western devotees, tupelo honey can be purchased in specialty markets, from gourmet catalogs, or online.

# Exotic Honeys from Around the World

## HONEY FROM THE LAND DOWN UNDER

Australia, once part of the ancient supercontinent of Gondwanaland, broke off from that land mass and was isolated from the rest of the world for millions of years. As a result, it has produced an abundance of nectar-rich plants that exist no place else on earth.

Since their introduction by European settlers in 1822, honey bees have done a good job keeping Aussie beekeepers supplied with fat frames of honey, ripe for extracting and packaging. Let's try some of the many different varieties.

### Jarrah Honey (*Eucalyptus marginata*)

Jarrah honey comes from the tallest tree in Australia, a prized hardwood that grows in the western forests of the continent. Some have described this honey as having a rich, full flavor reminiscent of coffee.

### Patterson's Curse Honey (*Echium plantagineum*)

Patterson's Curse, also known paradoxically as Salvation Jane, is a low-growing plant whose sky blue flowers carpet the countryside in summer and provide a wonderful crop of delicious honey. While beekeepers love the plant, Australian ranchers hate it since it can debilitate and even kill livestock that graze on its foliage. Happily, unlike the plant's leaves, the light amber, delicately flavored honey has no toxic properties. It is slow to crystallize, which gives it a long shelf life.

### Rough Bark Apple Honey (*Angophora bakeri*)

This honey is not from apple trees at all but from a tall species of eucalyptus, which flowers in December and January. Dark red, it has a strong, oaky flavor that leaves a slightly piquant but interesting aftertaste.

### Stringybark and Messmate Honeys (*Eucalyptus laevopinea* and other spp.)

These honeys come from a group of related eucalyptus trees native to New South Wales. They are very dark and full-bodied, with an aroma that has been compared to that of tanned leather. Fortunately, none of these honeys smells or tastes like eucalyptus leaves, the principal ingredient of Vicks VapoRub.

### Tasmanian Leatherwood Honey (Eucryphia lucida)

The island of Tasmania, off the southeast coast of Australia, got its first boatload of honey bees in 1831. Today, approximately two-thirds of its honey production comes from a native plant known as leatherwood. The rare leatherwood honey commands a high price and is much sought after by connoisseurs and gourmets. It is golden yellow, with an unusual, highly floral flavor, a piquant aroma, and a complex, lingering aftertaste. I always keep at least one jar of it in the honey cupboard of my kitchen. If you've never tasted leatherwood honey, give it a try. You'll probably add this honey to your top ten favorites list once you taste it.

# HONEY FROM THE LAND OF THE KIWI

Like Australia, the north and south islands of New Zealand were long isolated from the rest of the world. As a result, many of their nectar-producing plants are unique to the region.

### Kamahi Honey (Weinmannia racemosa)

The kamahi is a spreading tree with dark green, leathery leaves. A native of the temperate rain forest, it produces masses of creamy flowers that in turn yield a rich, amber-colored honey. Its full-bodied floral flavor has a buttery finish that lingers deliciously in the mouth.

### Manuka Honey (Leptospermum scoparium)

*Manuka* means "tea tree" in Maori, the language of the indigenous people of New Zealand. The honey ranges from creamy white to dark brown and is delicious, despite a hint of something slightly bitter and herbaceous. At $9,000 a ton, manuka honey may well be the world's most expensive.

The leaves of the manuka tree, which have strong anti-bacterial properties, have been used for centuries by the Maori as an effective treatment for wounds. Today, manuka honeys are being marketed in tubes and pre-coated sterile bandages as wound dressings. The types of manuka honey vary in their germ-fighting potency, but all have higher than normal activity against disease-causing microbes.

### Pohutukawa Honey (Metrosideros excelsa)

The pohutukawa tree with its brilliant red blossoms is also known as the New Zealand Christmas tree, since it flowers during the holiday season. Its honey is my personal favorite of all the New Zealand varieties, thick and creamy white, with a wonderful flavor that hints of butterscotch. The nectar of the pohutukawa blossoms was prescribed by Maori priests as a cure for sore throats.

# HONEY WITH A EUROPEAN ACCENT

### Lavender Honey (Lavandula angustifolia)

Lavender honey is world famous for its delicate floral bouquet and enchanting aroma, reminiscent of the scent of lavender in a sachet or potpourri mix. Experiencing this fine, imported honey, which is light amber and is often used in pastries and desserts, reminds many travelers of holidays spent driving or hiking through the lavender fields of Provence, where most of the world's limited supply comes from. (Lavender is widely cultivated in Provence to supply its large perfume industry.)

### Thyme Honey (Thymus vulgaris)

The modern Greeks are the world's largest producers of thyme honey, followed by Spain and France. While any honey can be flavored with a sprig of thyme, the real thing is made by honey bees from the nectar of thyme flowers and has an incomparably delicate flavor and aroma.

The ancient Greeks also had a taste for thyme honey. Solon, the Athenian legislator, complained that nearby Mount Hymettus was overcrowded with beekeepers and their hives, so he passed a law requiring that apiaries on the mountain be at least three hundred feet apart.

### Heather Honey (Calluna vulgaris)

A low-growing plant of the heaths, mountains, and moors, heather is a familiar sight in the northern and western regions of the British Isles. From its dense clusters of violet and purple blossoms, honey bees gather nectar and ripen it into one of the world's most fragrant and enticing honeys. It varies in color from deep amber to reddish brown and can have a gel-like consistency with an interesting bittersweet aftertaste.

## The Buzz at the Paris Opera

AS I MENTIONED earlier, beekeepers are an eccentric lot—none more so than a certain French beekeeper whose activities were reported in the *New York Times* on June 26, 2003.

Jean Paucton, then sixty-nine years young, is an urban apiculturist who keeps five weathered wooden hives on the roof of the Palais Garnier, the venerable opera house that stands as a landmark in the center of Paris. When he visits his charges, he dons his beekeeper's hood and a pair of heavy canvas gauntlets and climbs a narrow iron ladder to a parapet only two feet wide. On one side of the parapet, the roof falls away to the teeming streets of the city below. On the other side, a skylight slopes upward, its cracked panes evidence of visitors' struggles to keep their balance while fending off Paucton's bees.

Monsieur Paucton, a graphic artist who spent his career as a prop man for the opera, studied beekeeping at the

*The Palais Garnier*

Jardin du Luxembourg, where a school has been teaching Parisians about hive management for 150 years. Eighteen years ago, he ordered his first hive, which was delivered to him sealed and full of bees while he was still at work. He had intended to take it to his country place, but somehow the bees never left the opera. (A precedent had already been set by a colleague who raised trout in the opera's huge underground cistern.)

Today, his five hives, overlooking the elegant avenues of Paris, house about seventy-five thousand bees, which produce a thousand pounds of honey a year. Monsieur Paucton bottles and labels his Parisian honey at home, then sells it at the opera gift shop and at Fauchon, the world-famous gourmet specialty store.

According to Monsieur Paucton, his honey has a particularly intense floral flavor, thanks to the high concentration of flowering trees and shrubs that adorn the City of Light.

### Bell Heather Honey (*Erica cinerea*)

Nectar collected by bees from bell heather yields a full-flavored honey, often the surprising color of port wine. Hailing from the Scottish Highlands, bell heather is one of the emblems or plant badges used by Scottish clans.

### Chestnut Honey (*Castanea sativa*)

The European chestnut is especially common in northern Italy. Its honey is dark brown, similar to buckwheat honey in the United States. Like buckwheat honey, it has a taste some people love and others find quite unappealing. The flavor has been described as astringent, penetrating, and tannic, like that imparted to wine by the oak barrels in which it is aged.

### Strawberry Tree Honey (*Arbutus unedo*)

In Sardinia, strawberry tree honey is known as *miele amaro di corbezzolo,* the "honey beloved of honey bees." Reputed to have been a particular favorite of the Marquis de Sade, it has an almost intolerably bitter taste. The bright red fruit of this tree looks like strawberries from a distance. The Latin species name, *unedo,* means "I'll only eat one." Don't bother to look for this unusual honey on your local supermarket shelf—it won't be there.

### Canola Honey (*Brassica napus*)

Gone are the days when wildflowers blanketed hillsides and valleys across Europe. Today, much of the northern European countryside is a one-dimensional sea of yellow rapeseed, from which canola oil is made. Rapeseed honey is harvested by beekeepers in vast amounts and is often mixed with other honeys to soften its harsh, mustard-leaf flavor—not one of my favorites.

# It's Green,
# So How Can It Be Honey?

There are a few strange honeys you may come across, called honeydew honeys, that owe their existence to non-flowering plants. These honeys begin life as a sweet, sticky residue called honeydew, excreted by aphids that feed on pine needles. The honeydew falls to the ground, where it is found by bees who transform it into a pine green, highly flavorful honey. In France, this is called *miel de puce,* or "flea honey," and it is considered a great delicacy. In the Black Forest region of Germany, honeydew from another species of pine is gathered by bees and made into a honey known as forest or fir honey.

Another type of honeydew honey is produced in New Zealand by insects living in the crevices of tree bark. These insects secrete vast quantities of processed tree sap, which the ever-vigilant honey bees collect and take home to the honey factory. According to New Zealanders, honeydew honey is ideal for marinades and barbecue sauces.

In general, honeydew honeys have a very high mineral content and a pungent flavor that some have compared to cough medicine.

## Manna from Heaven

MANY OF US know that when the Israelites wandered the desert for forty years, they were sustained by manna from heaven. But no one really knows what manna actually was. One theory is that manna came from the honeydew produced by either aphids or scale insects living in the Holy Land. In Hebrew and Arabic, the word for honeydew is *man*, while *man-es-simma*, or manna, is "the honeydew that falls from the sky," which does give weight to the theory. Modern Jews especially enjoy honey as part of meals, along with apples, rice, spinach, tzimmes (an eastern recipe of honey-baked carrots), and even fish, during the Jewish New Year (the two-day celebration known as Rosh Hashanah). For them, honey signifies good living and wealth as well as being a symbol of fertility and abundance and spiritual renewal.

# Chapter 7

# Trading Honey in the Ancient and Modern Worlds

THE ROLE OF honey as food and medicine, as well as potent religious and political symbol, made it a highly lucrative item in world commerce. Everyone wanted honey, but not everyone could produce it—thus enter the honey merchants and traders, those savvy persons who satisfied the demand for honey by facilitating its journey from hive to market, thence to temple, apothecary, and cooking pot.

## Trading Honey in Ancient Cultures

### Egypt

People have been keeping bees and trading the honey they produce for thousands of years. The Egyptians, who were among the first to manage honey bees, transported their sweet cargoes on barges up and down the Nile. The importance of the honey trade in Pharaonic Egypt was

confirmed in 2002 at Saqqarah when archaeologists un-
earthed the opulent tomb of Ubi, the chief supervisor of
beekeepers. His was an important job, for the demand for
honey was great throughout the whole of the Egyptian
kingdom. It was used to sweeten many foods and beverages, was fed to sacrificial animals to sweeten the pleasure of the recipient god, and was used in medicines to
keep people alive and well. It was also associated with
love and romance, just as it is today. In one Egyptian
marriage contract, the groom pledged to give annual
gifts of honey to his bride, perhaps to sweeten the course
of conjugal life: *I take thee to wife . . . and promise to deliver to thee yearly twelve jars of honey.*

The amount of honey used was staggering. One record
indicates that Ramses III, whose reign lasted until 1153
BC, made gifts of 21,000 jars of honey to Hapi, the god of
the Nile, and ordered another 7,050 jars to be used in
making the honey cakes the deity was partial to. This
huge amount of honey required the total annual production of at least five thousand hives. When local supplies
fell short, honey was imported from Phoenicia, in modern Lebanon, and Canaan, the biblical land of milk and
honey in what is now Israel.

## Greece and Rome

The Greeks believed it was Dionysus, the god of wine,
who bestowed honey on humankind. Always enterprising, the Greeks made good use of this gift, successfully
trading honey throughout the classical world during the

fifth and fourth centuries BC, particularly with the Persians, Assyrians, and Phoenicians. At ports such as Piraeus, near Athens, they stored honey in barrels and loaded it onto merchant ships that crisscrossed the Mediterranean and Black seas, exchanging the honey, along with silver, olive oil, wine, and wheat, for cinnamon, pepper, silks, and timber. Honey played such a key role in Greek commerce that it was featured on coins along with the bee, a revered symbol of industriousness and efficiency. Honey bee images on coins were especially popular during the second century BC and were produced at the famous coin mint at Ephesus (now in modern Turkey).

*A silver tetradrachm coin, about the size of a U.S. quarter, struck at the mint in ancient Ephesus (modern Turkey). The coin was in circulation more than two thousand years ago (390–330 BC).*

Throughout the course of their empire, the Romans also minted and circulated coins that depicted the industrious honey bee, enabling people to purchase their favorite sweetener with money that featured its maker. Honey was the primary sweetener during Roman times, since sugar was unknown in the Mediterranean world. It was used in cooking and in preserving meat.

## The Arab World

By the seventh century AD, the Arabs, who had recently emerged from the deserts of what is now Saudi Arabia to conquer and convert much of the known world, were well established as the leading traders in the Middle East, North Africa, and most of eastern Asia. Baghdad, the capital of the Muslim caliphate, was the center of a culture noted for its great works of literature and philosophy as well as important scientific and mathematical discoveries. Arab merchants led caravans across the treacherous dunes of the Sahara Desert to barter citrus fruits, almonds, pistachios, saffron, and honey for the precious cakes of salt that were sold by the tribes of the West African Sahel. Honey was a key ingredient in many favorite Arab dishes, including pastries and roasted fowl adopted from the cuisine of the conquered Persians.

## China

The first evidence of organized beekeeping in China dates from the second century AD, considerably later than its establishment in the Mediterranean world. But even then, it was conducted on a relatively small scale, and most of the honey used in China for culinary and medicinal purposes was imported from the Mediterranean and the Middle East along the fabled Silk Road.

This great trading route, stretching from Byzantium in the West to China in the East, was actually a network of well-worn footpaths and rutted dirt roads connecting remote outposts and bustling markets in the far-flung regions of the ancient world. From the first century BC to the thirteenth century AD, when Marco Polo traveled it from Venice to the distant capital of the Mongol general Kublai Khan, camel and donkey caravans made their way along the Silk Road, crossing sun-scorched deserts and rugged, windswept mountains and encountering hostile tribes, rapacious bandits, and outlandish customs, all in the name of commerce.

Rice, sheep, dried fruit, tea, and wine traveled the Silk Road. Horses, glass, lacquer, cotton thread, ivory, gemstones, wool, and linen also went along for the ride. Honey was generally transported from the Mediterranean to China in dried gourds or bags made of animal skins like those used for wine. In Samarkand, an important stop on the Central Asian leg of the road, the Chinese bartered their highly prized silk for the highly prized food of the honey bee.

Not only did a myriad of goods travel the Silk Road, but culinary knowledge passed from region to region as well, introducing new flavors into old cultures as exotic spices were incorporated into local dishes. Many of these recipes called for honey, because the new, international menu featured honeyed wines, meats, and desserts.

## Central America

For at least two millennia, the Maya traded honey and beeswax along the routes that united their great cities throughout southern Mexico and Central America.

Honey, as we've already seen, was vital to the Maya not only as a cooking ingredient and medicine but also as an important part of many sacred rituals. Other goods traded included salt, ceramics, jade, obsidian (hard volcanic glass used in toolmaking), and the iridescent quetzal feathers that were prominently featured in their religious and royal paraphernalia.

## The Rise of Sugar and the Decline of the Honey Trade

Sugarcane is a giant grass native to the region of the Ganges delta in India. According to at least one legend, Buddha came from the land of sugar, called Gur, in present-day Bengal. When the Persian conqueror Darius the Great invaded the Indus Valley in 516 BC, he found the locals growing a "reed that gives honey without the aid of bees" and brought some samples home. Slowly, over the course of the following centuries, conquests by other foreign invaders as well as the Arab caravans that plied the Silk Road introduced sugarcane throughout the Middle East. However, it remained a relatively rare commodity both there and in Europe, so expensive that only the wealthiest could afford the "Indian salt."

Honey maintained its position as the primary sweetener until the early sixteenth century, when everything began to change. In 1506, Pedro d'Arranca brought sugarcane plants to the island of Santo Domingo (today's Dominican Republic), where sugar production became a major industry and soon spread throughout the West Indies. Grown by slaves on large plantations, sugar was cheaper and easier to produce and transport in large quantities than honey. By the seventeenth century, sugar had found its way into global commerce, and the volume of honey that was traded declined drastically.

While sugar was the major culprit in the decline of honey and the honey trade, it was not the only one. Honey had been used for healing purposes throughout the ancient world for thousands of years. But well before the introduction of cheap sugar, the therapeutic applications of honey had fallen out of favor among the physicians who had displaced traditional priests and shamans in the practice of medicine. It is difficult to say for sure why this happened, but by the Renaissance and the age of scientific enlightenment in the eighteenth century, honey was considered an old-fashioned folk remedy. New medicines and medical procedures began to emerge and, though primitive by modern standards, won the trust of the scientific community.

At nearly the same time that cheap sugar flooded the markets of Europe, supplies of honey began to dwindle. As human populations increased, so did the acreage they farmed and the cities and towns they inhabited, encroaching on traditional "bee pastures" and leaving bees with fewer and fewer foraging opportunities. Less nectar meant less honey, less honey meant higher prices, and higher prices meant an all-time low for the honey trade.

In the nineteenth century, beet sugar joined cane sugar

as a cheap sweetener, and the honey trade was dealt yet another serious blow, from which it would not recover until the latter half of the twentieth century.

## For the Best Honey, Go Local, Not Global

Unfortunately, most of us have yet to experience the rich flavor and evocative aromas of local, or "boutique," honeys purchased directly from beekeepers or at a farmers' market. As we saw in Chapter 6, there is an enormous and enticing variety of honey out there for you to discover and enjoy. In this age of globalization, however, the honey we find on our supermarket shelves has often come from halfway around the world, displacing the local and regional honeys that were once widely available. Blended with other honeys, these generic honeys have been robbed of any unique regional or floral identity. Transported in large steel drums by rail or in the bellies of freighters, they arrive at their destinations already past their prime.

But, like consumers everywhere, we can buck the trend by insisting on more food choices. Ask your store manager to stock tupelo, blueberry, orange blossom, eucalyptus, or other unblended honeys. Knowing where your food comes from can change your life. By searching out and buying local and regional honeys, you'll be supporting local beekeepers and small distributors as well as giving yourself an unforgettable treat.

# Chapter 8

# Searching for Gold: Ancient Rituals and Modern-Day Honey Hunters

WE WERE SITTING on a hillside above Pedu Lake in northern Peninsular Malaysia, listening to the mysterious, sometimes unnerving sounds of the rain forest and breathing in its damp, earthy smells. It was a hot, humid night in late February near the end of the rainy season, when the forest comes alive and entire tree crowns burst into riotous pink, blue, yellow, and green. Our group was an unusual mix of cultures, vocations, and interests. It included my longtime friend Paul Mirocha, an accomplished artist who frequently accompanies me on scientific expeditions; his sister, Julie, an independent filmmaker; several entomologists and evolutionary biologists; and a small party of ecotourists, some of whom had traveled halfway around the world to experience the events about to unfold. We had come together in the old-growth rain forest, with its skyscraper trees and leafy canopy, to witness a traditional Malaysian honey hunt.

We knew that similar honey hunts would be taking place that month in other areas of Peninsular Malaysia as well as in Sarawak, Borneo, Brunei, and Indonesia, all sharing a devotion to the fierce giant Asian honey bee (*Apis dorsata*), maker of a honey valued as much for its reputed healing properties as for its taste. Precious and in short supply, tualang honey (known by the name of the tree in which the bees make their nests) commands a much higher price than honey made by the Asian honey bee (*Apis cerana*) or even by the imported European honey bee (*Apis mellifera*). The men we would be watching that night risk their lives in pursuit of it.

Distant stars provided the only illumination as we waited on the hillside for the hunters to begin their ascent into the tualang tree, for there were no nearby cities to generate light pollution and no moon to dilute the darkness. An eclectic orchestra of insects and larger animals serenaded us. I was able to pick out the songs of stridulating male crickets, booming toads, trilling tree frogs, and katydids, but there were many other sounds within this rich and unrelenting cacophony that I could not identify. Not far from the spot where we were sitting stood the immense tualang tree where the hunt would take place. Draped with the nests of the giant bees, it soared 240 feet into the sky.

I shifted my weight and settled into the damp forest soil, trying to get comfortable in anticipation of the long hours ahead. Our guide, Dr. Makhdzir bin Mardan, a professor of zoology at the Universiti Putra Malaysia in Kuala Lumpur, sat beside us, as still and patient as I was eager. Even though this was not the first time I had been present at a Malaysian honey hunt, I could barely contain my excitement. The first honey hunt I had witnessed had been seven years earlier, when I had come to Pedu Lake for a conference on rain forest honey bees, and it had thrilled me so much that I had repeated the experience many times since.

On the morning of that first hunt, I'd hiked up the steep hill behind the lake to survey the site where the hunters would later be gathering for the night's events, and suddenly caught sight of a towering tualang tree. I knew that the tualang, with its fluted buttresses and smooth, white bark, is the tallest tree in all of Asia. But nothing had prepared me for the actual spectacle of the great tree, which rose 120 feet into the air before the first branches appeared, festooned with over one hundred bee colonies like living Christmas ornaments. A member of the species *Koompassia excelsa,* in the legume family, the tualang is actually a bean tree and would certainly be worthy of costarring in the tale of Jack and the Beanstalk. Only the enormous redwoods of northern California, and some eucalyptus in Australia, grow taller.

The giant honey bees that nest in the tualang trees are not permanent residents of the Pedu Lake region. Where they go during their long months away, neither the honey hunters nor modern bee researchers know exactly. They know only that *Apis dorsata* is a migratory species, always on the lookout for new sources of nectar as forest trees come into flower, then moving on when the bloom begins to wane. Migrating swarms are often seen flying high overhead to their mysterious destinations, moving across the skies like ominous clouds. But every November, they return to Pedu Lake to make and stockpile honey and to rear a new generation of giant bees.

*Giant single parabolic comb nests of the largest Asian honey bee* (Apis dorsata) *festoon a limb of the tualang tree at Pedu Lake, Malaysia.*

These bees are truly gorgeous insects. Their starkly contrasting colors never cease to amaze me. Bold bands of orange-brown, black, and white alternate at right angles to the long axis of their bodies. Their heads and legs are covered with black fuzz. Their wings are also black, with spectacular highlights of blue, purple, brown, and metallic gold, a shimmering palette that could have been created by an impressionist painter. When folded in repose over the backs of the bees, the paired black wings look like the capes of miniature Draculas.

Across the face of their giant honeycombs, six feet long

and shaped like half-moons, the bees form living, undulating blankets several layers deep. Beautiful as it is, this layering has a very practical purpose. Unlike the honey bees that we are familiar with in the United States, the giant bees of Asia don't live in tree cavities or other sheltering niches. Their massive but delicate wax combs are exposed to strong winds, intense monsoon downpours, and attacks from birds known as honey buzzards. The dense, interlocking layers of bees covering the surface of the vulnerable nest protect it, keeping the innermost bees, their larvae, stored pollen, and honey safe and dry.

It was during my first trip to Malaysia that I experienced what is perhaps the most startling behavior of the giant honey bees. I was peering through my binoculars at a colony high overhead when I realized that every few minutes the entire surface of the bee blanket covering the comb rippled outward from the center, in much the same way the surface of a pond ripples when a stone has been thrown into the water. It took less than a second for the ripples to reach the outermost edge of the four-foot-wide comb. I was mesmerized by the dazzling display of what appeared to be a perfectly synchronized communal dance. At the time, it was all a mystery to me. But recently, researchers have concluded that the bees create the ripple effect to dislodge parasitic flies and wasps that try to lay their eggs on the comb so their larvae can feed on the bee brood.

The honey-hunting expedition that had drawn us all to

the rain forest of Kedah province is part of a tradition that dates back to prehistoric times. Beginning with the reign of their first sultan, Muzaffar Shah I, who ruled from AD 1160 to 1179, the local honey-hunting clans have had to seek royal permission to raid the bee nests. Twenty-seven hereditary monarchs later, Muzaffar Shah's direct descendant, His Royal Highness Al-Sultan Almu'tasimu Billahi Muhibbuddin Tuanku Alhaj Abdul Halim Mu'adzam Shah, still has the authority to grant or refuse petitions from the honey hunters in his domain. He has this power because, as sultan, he technically owns everything in the forests.

Following the ritual that had been practiced by his ancestors for eight centuries, Pak Teh, the leader of the hunt we were about to witness, visited the royal palace back in 1965 to plead his case before the sultan. He had just located the bee trees near Pedu Lake and wanted to harvest their honey.

The result of that meeting in the 1960s was a formal letter issued by the sultan to Pak Teh granting his request to conduct honey hunts. Today, the sultan's letter, suitably framed, hangs in a place of honor inside Pak Teh's home in Jitra, near Alor Setar. It is one of his proudest possessions, he explained through an interpreter as he eagerly showed it to Paul Mirocha and me when we visited him during a previous trip to Malaysia. He went on to describe his audience at the palace nearly forty years before, his eyes still beaming at the recollection. When he had arrived at the gate, wearing his finest sarong, with a fresh turban coiled about his head, he was admitted by the guards and led to an elaborate room furnished with silk-cushioned sofas and chairs covered in gold leaf. There the sultan himself was waiting, resplendent in a blue silk tunic, his official robe of office, and the high-peaked royal turban with its jewel-encrusted ornamentation. The sultan's tunic was covered with large, gleaming medals, and his ceremonial dagger, thrust into his wide belt, hung by his side.

After the formal greetings, Pak Teh made his oral petition to the sultan, who in reply invited him to sit and describe a honey hunt. When Pak Teh finished speaking, the sultan smiled and gave him permission to harvest honey in the protected forest around Pedu Lake. Every year since then, a letter from the sultan has arrived at Pak Teh's home renewing his honey-hunting privileges—just as every year at the end of the hunt, Pak Teh returns to Alor Setar, where the sultan now lives in a new palace, to deliver a small amount of honey as tribute to the ruler.

The sultan's annual letter confirming Pak Teh's right to harvest the Pedu Lake honey arrived at his home two weeks before the hunt that we had come to witness. Not long after its arrival, Pak Teh began preparing for the event. Pak Teh is not only the leader of the honey hunt, but also the oldest member and leader of his clan. All of the other hunters are related to him: cousins, brothers-in-law, nephews, and grandsons. He is a compact, wiry man, with a quick, easy smile and a bald head wrapped in a turban fashioned from a towel. When not planning and leading honey hunts, he keeps busy as a rice farmer, a rubber planter, a carpenter, and the Imam of his neighborhood mosque.

Pak Teh and the other members of the clan spent several days checking and repairing their equipment—the climbing ropes, honey containers, leather buckets, bone knives, and liana torches they would need for a successful harvest. (Liana torches are made from sturdy vines that colonize the rain forest trees. After being pounded with knives and reduced to soft, pliable fibers, the lianas are bound into six-foot-long bundles about four inches thick. Each torch can burn for an entire night.) A week before the hunt was to begin, the hunters packed the equipment into their old blue minivan and set out on their journey. The team was made up of Pak Teh, four other adult men, and Pak Teh's two teenage grandsons, Shukor and Nizam, who, in an important rite of passage, were going to be initiated into the honey-hunting rituals.

When they reached the rain forest site an hour later, the hunters set up camp about fifteen minutes downhill from the bee tree, next to a small, clear stream. They hung a large blue plastic tarpaulin from a rope strung between two trees to serve as their roof, then spread a blanket on the ground below the tarp. A few sheets and pillows made up their simple beds. Lashed railings fashioned from cut saplings provided walls for their temporary home. They then unpacked their cooking pots, plates, and utensils and arranged them on the rocks that formed the campfire circle, a semipermanent installation used year after year. Finally, the hunters dammed part of the stream to create a pool for bathing.

The low-growing plants near the camp were spotted with thousands of small yellow dots, remnants of feces the bees released on their evening flights out of the nearby nests. On an earlier trip, I had collected some of this material and analyzed the pollen grains it contained in order to identify which flowers the secretive bees had visited high in the forest canopy. On this trip, I was planning to collect honey and pollen from the combs as well as a new supply of bee feces to analyze for pollen back home in Tucson.

Pak Teh was optimistic about the upcoming harvest. Ever since the bees had returned from their annual migration the previous November, he had been making occasional visits to the rain forest, hiking to the bee trees to observe how many colonies had arrived and how the flowering season was progressing. In this way, he was able to predict whether the harvest would be bountiful or not. Happily, this year his predictions were encouraging.

Once they were established at the camp, the seven honey hunters devoted most of their time to replacing sections of the old ladder that was attached to the bee tree. The humidity of the rain forest as well as hordes of voracious termites had taken their toll on the structure, making it unsafe. The men used nails to reanchor the ladder to the tree trunk and reinforced the crosspieces with saplings and rattan, which had been gathered in the forest. After nearly a week of hard work, all the equipment had been readied, the climbing ropes neatly coiled, and the large leather and rattan buckets scrubbed and placed conveniently at hand. To facilitate the raising and lowering of the honey buckets, a wooden pulley had been secured to the underside of a massive limb 120 feet up in the tualang tree.

After a long hike from the main road, our group had arrived at the forest camp on the afternoon of the day the hunt was to begin. With several hours of light left, we were able to watch the hunters as they made a final check of their nylon ropes and long, tightly bundled liana torches. As evening approached, Makhdzir bin Mardan cleared his throat and prepared to tell us about the traditions governing the honey harvest so that we would better understand the ceremonies we were about to witness. Professor Mardan had become an expert in the honey hunt through repeated trips to these forests. Born in Malaysia but educated at Guelph University in Canada, he is a slender man with glasses, black hair, and a thin goatee, as much at home in the rain forest with the giant bees as he is on campus and in lecture halls.

Out of the vast store of tales filed away in his memory, Makhdzir chose the ancient fable describing the origins of honey hunting in this part of the world.

"Long ago," he began, "a princess of the royal family had a Hindu handmaiden, a dusky beauty called Hitam Manis or 'Sweet Dark One.' The handmaiden fell hopelessly in love with the sultan's son, a handsome prince who requited her passion. But their love was doomed, for she was a commoner, and marriage of a commoner to a prince of the blood was strictly forbidden. When the sultan learned of the romance, he flew into a rage, and Hitam Manis, along with the other handmaidens, the Dayang, had to flee the palace for their very lives. As the terrified young women escaped into the forest, they were pursued by the sultan's guards, who hurled long metal spears at them. When one of the spears pierced the already broken heart of Hitam Manis, miraculously she did not die. Instead, she and the other handmaidens were transformed into a swarm of bees and disappeared into the night. Thus were born the giant honey bees of the Asian rain forests."

*Hitam Manis transformed into a swarm of bees and disappeared into the night.*

Pausing in his story, the professor suggested that we lie down on the forest floor and look up into the canopy of the tualang tree in anticipation of what would happen next in the story of Hitam Manis.

"Years later, the still grieving prince—now engaged to a proper princess—noticed a large honeycomb high in the branches of a tualang tree in the forest. When he climbed the tree to investigate, he discovered a large cache of golden honey. He called down for his servants to send up a metal knife and bucket so he could harvest the treasure. The servants dutifully sent the knife and bucket up to the prince, but when they lowered the now heavy pail a few minutes later, to their shock and horror they found the prince's dismembered body inside.

"From the treetops, a ghoulish voice cried out that he had committed a sacrilege by cutting the honeycomb with a sharp metal knife. Unwittingly, the prince had insulted poor Hitam Manis, reminding her of the cold metal spear that had pierced her heart and so changed her life. But the Sweet Dark One took pity on the prince she had once loved, and released a golden shower that restored him to life and limb."

Professor Mardan went on to explain that "golden showers"—which leave thousands of yellow spots on the forest foliage like those found near the honey hunters' base camp—are actually mass defecations made by *Apis dorsata* during their flights after sunset, when they rid themselves of feces and unwanted heat. A search for evidence of biological warfare in Southeast Asia occurred in 1979 and into the 1980s in Vietnamese and Laotian Hmong villages. The incidents and symptoms suggested the use of biological toxins called mycotoxins. There was confusion between "golden showers" and the new term "yellow rain," a phenomenon that was suspected of poisoning Hmong villagers. Scientists knew that golden showers are a natural part of bee biology—and an ecologically valuable contribution to the environment. They are distinct from the biological warfare used on the Hmong people during the Vietnam War. Malay farmers consider themselves lucky to have fields or rice paddies near a bee tree. It is a good omen to have the bees living nearby. The farmers understand that the daily cleansing flights deposit large amounts of nitrogen- and pollen-rich feces on their crop lands.

"To this day," Makhdzir concluded, "in deference to the dying anguish of the handmaiden known as Hitam Manis, honey hunters never use tools made of metal—only those of wood, cowhide, and bone."

*Pak Teh the honey hunter in front of his hundred-year-old wooden home in the town of Jitra. He holds a bone knife and a leather bucket used to collect honey from* Apis dorsata.

PHOTO BY PAUL MIROCHA

And so it is that Pak Teh and the other honey hunters of his clan use leather buckets, and knives made from the shoulder bone of a cow.

In the early evening, not long after Professor Mardan had recounted the Hitam Manis story, Pak Teh assembled his hunters in a semicircle at the edge of the camp. As our group watched from a respectful distance, he gave instructions to the four climbers, who included his grandsons Nizam and Shukor, and then to the two older men who would serve as the ground crew, sending buckets up to receive the giant beeswax combs and lowering them to be emptied when they were full.

Next, Pak Teh cupped his large, strong bronzed hands around a smoky oil lamp and uttered an ancient prayer, the same one he had been reciting in this very spot for nearly forty years. We couldn't understand the dialect of Bahasa Melayu spoken in this border region, but that didn't matter, since the words were not meant for our ears. In fact, it was forbidden for us to hear what was being said. We were not members of the honey-hunting clan, nor had we earned the right to participate in their ancient rituals. We were outsiders.

Makhdzir explained to us that Pak Teh was asking the bee tree, the forest spirits, and the giant bees themselves for permission to make the night's climb and for a successful harvest. His words were drawn from Islamic and Hindu prayers as well as animist beliefs dating back to the time when only the indigenous Orang Asli tribes lived in these forests. We could imagine ancient Orang

Asli honey hunters uttering similar prayers thousands of years ago, long before the coming of Pak Teh's people, not to mention the nosy bee scientists and ecotourists from half a world away.

After Pak Teh had finished the ritual prayers, our group was led from the base camp to the bee tree clearing on the hillside. Because night had already fallen, we didn't have to worry about the bees—they couldn't see us in the darkness. People who visit bee trees during the day, however, have to walk slowly and use the branches of tall shrubs to hide their movements. Anyone who doesn't take such precautions is likely to suffer countless stings delivered by the nest's fierce guardians. In fact, it is not uncommon for people to be hospitalized as a result of these massive, sometimes fatal attacks. Still, despite the risks, the Malay honey hunters always refer to the giant honey bees with great tenderness. They call the bees Hitam Manis, a lover worthy of a royal prince. During the hunt, they humbly refer to themselves as Dayang, the palace handmaidens of legend. The few times I observed Pak Teh being stung, he always smiled as he gently brushed off the offending bees. As far as he was concerned, he might have been getting bee kisses from his fine friends, instead of painful stings from the world's largest and fiercest honey bee species.

We were lucky that there was no moon on the night of our hunt. On nights with a moon, the hunters have to wait until after it has set to avoid detection by the resting but ever-vigilant bees. Now, as we watched from our hillside vantage point, Pak Teh and his fellow climbers quickly started their ascent with coiled ropes slung over their shoulders. They climbed the ladder barefoot, wearing loose clothing with no Western-style veils or protective beekeeping equipment. Shukor trailed the long liana torches from a cord attached to his waist. The hunters climbed in silence and without flashlights until they reached a height of more than one hundred feet. (Flashlights might alarm the bees and set off a defensive attack.) The first-level branches were four or five feet in diameter. Beneath them hung the massive combs, each six feet long, four feet wide, and fat with honey. Both sides of the combs were covered with striped bees in interlocking layers five or six deep.

It was a familiar climb for Pak Teh, who had been harvesting honey from the Pedu Lake bee trees every year since 1965. Now, with his eyesight failing due to cataracts, he was eagerly training his grandsons in the important traditions of the honey harvest. Though this was their first hunt, Nizam and Shukor were scrambling up into the branches of the tree with as much agility and fearlessness as their much more experienced elders. The rest of us sat below on the damp hillside, waiting and listening for any sounds from above.

During my first visit seven years earlier, I had hammed it up, bravely climbing the ladder a modest fifteen or twenty feet for photo opportunities to impress friends and family back in Tucson. Climbing the rest of the way up to the bee nests was unimaginable. The honey hunters, however, are much braver. They scamper up the sturdy but frail-looking ladder with remarkable speed, seeming entirely at ease with this death-defying feat.

When they reached their precarious treetop destinations, it was time for the harvest to begin. Pak Teh's voice rang out as he announced that he was poised on a branch immediately above a bee nest, ready to cut the honeycomb. But before the comb could be cut and folded into the leather bucket, the bees would have to be evicted from their home—a process that involved the clever use of both fire and song. Fifty feet from where our group was sitting, Pak Teh's brother-in-law waited at the base of the tree. Now, in a loud, clear voice, he began to chant, calling to the tree, the stars, the spirits of the forest, and the bees themselves in their lofty nests. His voice rang strong and true through the moist, hot air of the tropical night. Even the noisy insects seemed to grow quiet when he sang his song of Hitam Manis.

> *"Hitam Manis Ooooi!"*
> *(Sweet Dark One, Ooooi!)*
> *"Turunlah dengan chahaya bintang"*
> *(Come down with the falling stars)*
> *"Turun dengan lemah lembutnya"*
> *(Come down gracefully)*

*A herringbone ladder snakes its way 120 feet up into the boughs of the tualang tree climbed by Pak Teh and his honey-hunter clan. Pedu Lake, Malaysia.*

When Shukor passed the burning liana torch to his grandfather, we saw its glowing tip arc through the still night air. Soon a cascade of orange embers rained down like a meteor shower from the branches overhead. No Fourth of July fireworks display has ever been so memorable for me. It is a pyrotechnic spectacle that has kept me returning to the bee trees of Pedu Lake seven times so far.

As the first orange sparks floated lazily to the ground, I heard an ominous roar from above. The inhabitants of Pak Teh's colony were flying in our direction—tens of thousands of incensed bees following the rain of fire earthward. On my first honey hunt years before, I had instinctively ducked and huddled in the darkness, shaken by the prospect of imminent attack and convinced that the bees would easily find me. But now I knew there was nothing to fear. Long ago in these ancient forests, honey hunters learned how to manage the bees, using the sparks from burning liana torches. The bees followed the drifting trails of glowing sparks to the ground. The roar of the oncoming "bee locomotive" ended as abruptly as it had started as the bees settled harmlessly on the vegetation below. The bees would be unable to find their way home or attack the honey hunters until the morning light. But by then the hunters would be safely out of the tree.

Pak Teh's brother-in-law repeated the chant to Hitam Manis whenever he saw sparks spilling from the torches above, the signal that the climbers were driving the bees from yet another nest. The distinctive rhythm of the chant mesmerized us, filling the tree clearing as it cajoled the bees to leave their colonies high in the tualang branches.

As the honey hunt proceeded, the giant waxen combs were cut from the tree branches, folded into halves or quarters, and sent down in the leather buckets to the two men waiting on the forest floor. After the buckets had been emptied and sent back up to be refilled, the combs were squeezed through funnels covered with cheesecloth into two immense blue plastic containers, each holding perhaps a hundred liters of honey. Finally, at about four a.m., after seven hours in their treetop workplace, the climbers made their way down to solid ground, having collected honey from a dozen or more colonies. (Each night for a week they would climb again into the tualang tree until over a thousand pounds of honey had been harvested from perhaps eighty colonies.) Visibly exhausted from the long night's exertions, the hunters nonetheless had an air of exhilaration about them, the look of men who know that they have successfully completed a particularly difficult job.

But Pak Teh still had one more important task to perform. Standing at the foot of the towering tree as the rising sun began to color the sky a brilliant crimson, he prepared to carry out yet another time-honored ritual. As his weary men looked on, he carefully selected a large honeycomb from those in the honey bucket. Lifting it, he uttered something we couldn't hear, then hurled the comb deep into the forest behind the tree. Makhdzir explained that this, the first honey taken, was an offering to the "unseen owner" of the forest and its trees, given in thanks for yet another safe and bountiful harvest.

Our group now joined Pak Teh and the others under an immense boulder overhang where, tired and hungry, we all huddled around the sticky harvest to partake in a ritual meal of honey and brood. It was a joyous celebration of the life-giving nectar and pollen of the forest. Some of us vied for the tastiest morsels, letting the honey drizzle down our throats, then spitting out the indigestible chunks of beeswax. Pak Teh handed me a piece of comb heavy with white bee grubs peeking out of their cells and urged, *"Makan, makan"* ("Eat, eat"). Not wanting to offend him, I tasted the plump bee larvae. My UC Davis graduate studies had taught me that honey bee larvae make a wonderful quiche, and I now discovered they weren't bad raw on the half comb.

Meanwhile, under the boulder overhang, the men from Jitra continued to laugh and joke as they filtered honey into the big blue plastic containers. In a few days they would break camp and drive out of the Pedu Lake forest. Back home, they would have another ritual feast with their families and friends. Once again they would give thanks to the forest and its majestic bees. And then they would divide the honey among themselves, keeping some for their own use, then bottling and selling the rest in neighboring markets or to the local honey cooperative.

Honey hunting is in the blood of Pak Teh and the others of his clan. What seems to us like the most dangerous of pursuits is an event that they look forward to and cherish each year. While the supplemental income from selling the tualang honey is important, what matters most is the special relationship they have with the rain forest bees.

After the hunt was over and the men had returned to their homes, Paul, Julie, and I visited Pak Teh's home to photograph the clan and sample more of the marvelous tualang honey. Built over one hundred years ago by Pak Teh's father with termite- and rot-resistant rain forest timber, the house is the oldest building in the oldest part of town. It is held together with wooden pegs and rises eight feet above the ground on sturdy wooden stilts, insurance against the monsoon floods that frequently inundate the region. The wooden walls and roof beams have been elaborately hand-carved with intricate geometric and floral patterns. The weather-beaten old house sits proudly in a big garden planted with lush fruit-bearing trees.

Before leaving Jitra, we asked Pak Teh if honey hunting would continue into the future. After all, during this hunt, his grandsons had been literally handed the torch. In response to the question, Pak Teh just smiled and uttered the soft, pleasing laugh we had heard so often during the past few days.

"As long as there are tualang trees in the forests," he said, "and giant bees to build nests in them, there will be hunters like us to harvest their honey."

## Honey Hunting in the Shadow of the Himalayas

Modern-day honey hunts that carry on ancient rituals and traditions are not confined to the rain forests of Malaysia. Honey is still harvested by intrepid hunters in many far-flung parts of the world, from the valleys of Nepal to the homeland of the Australian Aborigines.

In Nepal, our friends the giant honey bees build their nests not in towering trees but on sheer cliffsides to discourage predation by honey-hungry humans and other animals. Situated at the base of the Himalayas, Nepal provides an abundance of these seemingly impregnable nesting sites. But even so, there is no guarantee that the bees' refuge won't be breached by human ingenuity, daring, and greed, as has been happening for thousands of years.

Many men of the Gurung tribe, who live in the foothills of the Himalayas in west central Nepal, still practice the art of the traditional honey hunt, risking life and limb as they dangle on rope ladders high above the ground to loot the giant combs attached to the cliffside.

Although no historical records exist, Gurung honey hunts have almost certainly been taking place for millennia, with generation after generation of hunters passing their ancient skills on to their sons, teaching them all they need to know, from how to perform the ritual offerings that will protect them from danger and death to the correct way to light and maintain the smoky fires that will pacify the fierce bees.

Each nest yields from 135 to 160 pounds of honey and beeswax, both of which are valuable commodities in the marketplace. The Nepalese use honey not only as food but also as a universal remedy, believed to be good for whatever ails you. It is sold to villagers or exchanged for other products, such as milk, yogurt, grain, or perhaps a chicken. The wax too has its uses, for many artisans in Kathmandu still practice the ancient art of lost-wax casting when making religious figurines and are eager to purchase the hunters' stock.

While Nepalese honey hunts are still a viable source of

both honey and income (not to mention adventure) for the impoverished villagers, I can't help wondering how many more there will be. As in Malaysia and so many other parts of the world, the forests of Nepal are shrinking rapidly as more and more wood is cut for fuel and building materials. And when the trees disappear, the torrential monsoon rains, with nothing to block their way, gush down the hillsides, washing away both meadows filled with wildflowers and terraced paddies, important sources of nectar and pollen for the bees. As their raw materials dwindle, compromising their ability to produce honey, increasing numbers of bees are abandoning their cliffside dwellings and relocating in parts unknown. How long the others will remain is a question no one can answer.

## The Sugarbag Quest: Honey Hunting in Northern Australia

For thousands of years, the Aborigines of Australia have survived in a landscape whose harsh conditions would have broken the spirit of many other peoples. In scrubby, sun-baked deserts, they learned how to harvest what they needed from a seemingly ungiving natural world—and one of the things they needed was honey. Like all the other human inhabitants of our planet, Aborigines have a serious sweet tooth, and to satisfy it, they have long robbed honey from the nests of their native bees, particularly stingless bees of the genera *Trigona* and *Austroplebeia*. Unlike Pak Teh's clan and their Nepalese counterparts, the Aborigines don't have to worry about attacks from guard bee defenders of the nests they are violating, for bees without stingers are much less formidable than their well-armed relatives.

Aborigines use the English word *sugarbag* to refer to both the hardworking stingless bees and the honey and resins they loot from the bees' nests. The honey plays an important role in their diet, improving the flavor of many foods and providing a sweet drink when mixed with water.

"Dreamtime" or creation stories told by tribal elders around campfires help Aborigines reaffirm their connection to the past as well as to the natural world in which they live. Honey bee dreaming is a repository of the traditions that govern the ways humans think of and interact with honey bees.

# Chapter 9

# Good for What Ails You

IN THE CLASSIC movie *Mary Poppins,* a song explains that "a spoonful of sugar helps the medicine go down." I would go a step further: Not only will honey make the medicine go down better than sugar, it is actual medicine. From our earliest history down to the present day, people have been fortifying themselves and curing diseases and infections with honey. While some of its medicinal uses have fallen out of favor and been discredited as mere fads, others have actually been shown to produce genuine therapeutic results. In fact, modern scientists are actively studying a wide range of new medicinal applications for honey.

I am not suggesting that you move honey from your kitchen pantry to your medicine cabinet. But it is fascinating how, across cultures, our age-old bond with bees hasn't just sweetened our lives but has healed our bodies as well.

# The Germ-Killing Properties of Honey

There is no doubt that honey is an effective antibiotic. Why? The answer is short and sweet: sugar. Honey is roughly 80 percent sugars and 20 percent water (plus a few minor ingredients). The sugars are what make honey such a quick energy booster. But can they really kill most of the rogue's gallery of bacteria and fungi that infect our world? Well, yes, they can. It's all about something called osmotic pressure. Osmosis is the movement of a solvent through a semipermeable membrane into a solution of higher concentration. The high sugar content of honey, along with its natural acidity, creates a very unpleasant habitat for single-celled microbes. These troublesome little creatures come encased in a thin, semipermeable membrane through which water is able to pass. Think of a bacterium as a water balloon sitting in honey. Thanks to the osmotic pressure exerted by the honey's highly concentrated sugars, the water molecules in the bacterium, essential to its survival, are drawn through the thin membrane into the honey. With the help of a high-power microscope, you can actually see the bacterium shrinking before your eyes. The story doesn't have a happy ending for the dehydrated microbes, which, unable to withstand the osmotic pressure, simply shrivel up and die.

Osmotic pressure isn't the only reason honey is an effective antibiotic. It also kills bacteria because it contains hydrogen peroxide. Glucose oxidase is an enzyme secreted by bees when they convert nectar into honey. In the presence of oxygen, the enzyme splits glucose molecules into water and hydrogen peroxide. Full-strength honey has very low amounts of hydrogen peroxide and not much active glucose oxidase. When it's diluted, however, a huge increase in enzyme activity occurs. This makes honey a slow-release antiseptic, one that does not damage tissue as other antiseptics sometimes can. Modern laboratories around the world have tested the killing power of honey against a number of bacterial pathogens, with deadly results to the infection-causing bugs. While pharmaceutical companies have yet to produce honeyed antibiotics, bandages impregnated with honey are already used in Europe, Australia, and New Zealand to help prevent wounds from becoming infected.

Although the ancients didn't have microscopes to observe the potent antibacterial properties of honey, through trial and error they learned that if they applied honey and grease, or honey alone, to wounds, they healed faster and didn't get infected. Amazing.

## Healing with Honey
## Through the Ages

We do not know the exact sequence of events, but early in our past, we came to rely on honey as a medicine with a wide range of benefits.

One prescription for the wonder drug of the ancients is

found in the Vedas, the sacred Hindu books compiled between 1500 and 500 BC: *Let one take honey . . . to beautify his appearance, develop his brain, and strengthen his body.* We have to wait until much later for the first written instructions for the preparation of a honeyed healing agent: *Grind to a powder river dust . . . then knead it in water and honey and let plain oil and hot cedar oil be spread over it.* Scratched in cuneiform onto the surface of a baked clay tablet, this Sumerian prescription has been interpreted by scholars as the recipe for an unguent to treat disorders of the ears and eyes. Other Sumerian writings from that period refer to honey mixed with butter or other animal fats to form a greasy paste used to heal pierced earlobes and surgical incisions.

The early Egyptians also appreciated honey's healing properties, raiding their cylindrical clay beehives to treat a host of medical complaints. Their honey prescriptions appeared not on the clay tablets used by the Sumerians but on papyrus, a durable parchment paper made from reeds that grew in the extensive marshes along the banks of the Nile. A large number of these papyrus records have been recovered from tombs and deciphered by modern Egyptologists. One of the most famous is the Ebers Papyrus, among the oldest medical texts to have been found in Egypt, dating from about 1550 BC. It contains recipes for medicinal preparations as well as instructions for physicians on how to use them. Out of 700 formulas, 147 call for honey as one of the principal healing agents. To cure baldness, physicians were advised to concoct a mixture of ground red ocher, powdered alabaster, and honey.

The Edwin Smith Papyrus (named for the man who purchased it along with the Ebers Papyrus in 1862) details forty-eight possible uses for honey as a healer. This is one of them.

Case Two: Instructions concerning a gaping wound in the head, penetrating to the bone

*To examine a man having a gaping wound in the head penetrating to the bone, you should lay your hand on the wound and palpate it. If you find the skull is uninjured, not having a perforation in it, you should bind fresh meat to the wound with two strips of linen to draw the wound together, then treat it with grease and honey every day thereafter until he recovers.*

This sounds a bit gross, doesn't it? The Egyptian physician who wrote this case knew what he was talking about. As we have already seen, the antibacterial properties of honey help prevent wounds from becoming infected. The Egyptian physician was right on, since honey's effectiveness as an anti-inflammatory has been confirmed by modern research.

The Smith Papyrus also explained how to treat burns with linen bandages soaked in honey, an area modern researchers have studied with positive results. Malachite, a form of copper carbonate, was pulverized and mixed with honey to cure conjunctivitis, a common eye infection.

The same mixture was used in eye makeup, a cosmetic the Egyptians applied lavishly, as evidenced in their stylized tomb paintings. Imagine—an eye makeup that doubles as a cure for eye infections. The ingenious Egyptians also used honey as a laxative for chronic constipation.

During the Tang Dynasty (AD 618 to 907), beeswax was used to make pills easier to swallow, while bee stings were found effective in treating arthritis, a theory that is being tested in medical labs today. But it was honey, not beeswax or stings, that had the widest-ranging medicinal applications. In the treatment of smallpox, honey was rubbed all over the patient's body to stop the progression of the disease and help prevent scarring.

Even in modern China, most of the honey produced is used for medicinal purposes, such as the treatment of fluid deficiency, blood disorders, constipation, sore throat, and a general feeling of weakness. Many medicinal herbs are powdered, then mixed with honey as a binder to form pills. Taking a page from the Tang, the pills are then coated with beeswax. Some medicinal roots and leaves are stir-fried with honey to increase their efficacy.

In the fourth century BC, Democritus, known as the "laughing philosopher," credited honey for his long and healthy life—he laughed his way through a reputed 109 years.

In the Roman pharmacopoeia, honey was often prescribed alone or in combination with herbal ingredients. According to such scholarly sources as Pliny the Elder (AD

23–79), the Romans believed honey cured maladies of the throat and mouth as well as pleurisy, pneumonia, and even snakebite. Pliny himself suggested that honey mixed with the sap of aloe was an effective treatment for bruises, burns, and abrasions. Pliny's contemporary, Dioscorides, creator of *De Materia Medica,* the five-volume Roman equivalent of our medical *Physicians' Desk Reference,* was a great believer in honey as an agent of good health. Among other things, he recommended it for sunburn, ulcers, inflammations of the tonsils, and cough, and as an effective way to kill body and head lice and nits.

## Alexander's Final Journey

Not only did the ancients believe honey saved lives, but they may also have used it to embalm bodies from which life had departed. The ancient Aryans, Babylonians, Sumerians, Egyptians, and Cretans are all thought to have buried their great men in honey since honey not only conferred immortality but was a great preservative, thanks to its powerful antibacterial qualities. It has long been said that the corpse of Alexander the Great was embalmed in honey so it could make the long, arduous journey from the shores of the Euphrates River, where he died, to its final, faraway resting place.

Alexander the Great had conquered the known world by age thirty-three. After a night of revelry in the ancient palace of Nebuchadnezzar on the banks of the Euphrates, Alexander was taken sick. It may have been a matter of too much unmixed wine or a dose of poison administered by a jealous rival. After ten days of feverish delirium, Alexander the Great, master of the world's mightiest realm, was no more.

According to a popular and enduring legend, the young king's ravaged body was embalmed in liquid honey, then placed in a massive sarcophagus of pure gold amid the mourning of his men and the keening of his women. Honey would have been the perfect agent to prevent the decomposition of the body as it traveled across the deserts of the Middle East. Because of honey's osmotic properties, it literally sucks the life out of bacteria that cause dead flesh to decay.

# The Use of Honey
# in Modern Medicine

Between 200 BC and AD 400, countless texts were written about the therapeutic advantages of honey, often recording discoveries made during the previous two thousand years. Yet despite its widespread use as a healing agent by the ancients, the curative properties of honey were largely forgotten by medical practitioners after the fall of the Roman Empire. We know of only one text, *The Leech Book of Bald,* written between AD 924 and 946 by an English monk named Bald, that recommends honey as a medicine, in this case as an eye salve and wound treatment (two uses being investigated by modern researchers). Virtually nothing was written about the medical attributes of honey during the Dark and Middle Ages, periods of intellectual stagnation in many disciplines.

With the coming of the Renaissance, however, there was a sporadic revival of interest in honey as medicine. An anonymous treatise written in 1446 describes a seven-step regimen for ulcer care, using a multitude of ingredients that include honey, beeswax, white wine, and red cabbage leaves. In 1623, an English minister, the Reverend Charles Butler, published *The Feminine Monarchie,* an important treatise on the lives and ways of honey bees. In the book, he promoted the use of honey as a disinfectant, cough medicine, eye salve, calming potion for gastric upsets, restorative drink, and laxative. Interestingly, all of these uses of honey are being studied today. In 1759, Dr. John Hill wrote a book whose title says it all: *The Virtues of Honey in Preventing Many of the Worst Disorders and in the Certain Cure to Several Others: Particularly the Gravel, Asthmas, Coughs, Hoarseness, and a Tough Morning Phlegm.* The opening paragraph of this worthy book laments the fact that honey had fallen out of favor in medical practice:

*The slight regard at this time paid to the medical virtues of Honey is an instance of the neglect men shew to common objects, whatever their value ... we seek from the remotest part of the world medicines of harsh and violent operation for our relief in several disorders under which we should never suffer if we would use what the bee collects for us at our doors.*

During the nineteenth century, as more and more pharmaceuticals became available, the use of honey in health care nearly ceased altogether. People wanted modern medicines developed by modern scientists in modern labs. Few believed that the old folk remedies of their grandparents and great-grandparents had any real curative powers. In Europe and America, honey was used merely as a sweetener to help bitter chemical medicines go down. It was also added to the herbal or mud poultices that were applied to wounds—and was surely the best ingredient in the mix, the only one with actual anti-infection efficacy.

In the twenty-first century, however, medicinal honey has begun to make a comeback as new clinical studies confirm many of the ancient healing powers of our favorite sweetener. A few of these studies are summarized here to give you an idea of the current status of honey as part of the modern medical equipment and references used by doctors.

## Honeyed Bandages for the Treatment of Severe Wounds and Burns

When it comes to antibacterial properties, clinical researchers have found that all honeys are not created equal. Most inhibit bacterial growth to some degree, due to their high osmolarity and the bacteria-hating hydrogen peroxide they produce. But only some honeys are potent enough to actually stop bacterial growth. One of the most powerful antibacterial honeys is manuka from New Zealand. Manuka contains phytochemicals derived from the nectar of certain plants that manuka-making bees visit during their foraging expeditions. This, added to the osmotic pressure and hydrogen peroxide, makes it one of the honeys that bacteria don't want to encounter. Clinical trials in Australia and New Zealand have used manuka-impregnated dressings to produce remarkable results in infected wounds and ulcers that had been unresponsive to conventional antibiotics. One study reported that manuka dressings successfully resolved a surgical wound that had failed to heal over a period of thirty-six months, during which it was treated with both systemic and topical antibacterials as well as three surgical procedures. After being dressed with manuka bandages, however, the wound was completely healed in just one month.

Not only have manuka and other honeys been found to resolve persistent infections, they also clean and deodorize wounds and reduce pain, inflammation, and the level of exudate (the moisture that wounds emit, which can undermine the efficacy of topical treatments by diluting them).

Honey has been found particularly helpful in treating severe burns when it's applied to the dressing that covers the wound. (The Egyptians figured this one out about thirty-five hundred years ago.) Because they will not stick to the burn during scab formation, honey-impregnated dressings prevent the painful irritation caused by traditional dressings that adhere to the burned tissue. This, in turn, allows faster tissue regeneration and promotes skin growth.

As more and more bacteria become resistant to conventional antibiotics, honey is gaining broader acceptance as a therapy for difficult-to-heal wounds and burns that haven't responded to pharmaceuticals. In 2001, two honey-impregnated dressings came on the market for the treatment of severe burns and unresponsive wound infections. HoneySoft, manufactured by a Dutch company, is a patented plaster that contains a modern healing agent (ethylene vinyl acetate, or EVA, a medical glue) and pure high-grade honey free of pollutants. In one clinical trial, HoneySoft was used to dress sixteen traumatic wounds, twenty-three complicated surgical wounds, and twenty-one chronic, nonresponding wounds. All but two of the wounds had successfully healed in a mean time of three weeks (range one to twenty-eight weeks).

In Australia, New Zealand, the Netherlands, and to a lesser extent the United Kingdom, honey-impregnated dressings are now being used in many private and state hospitals. Though not yet available in the United States, which frequently lags behind other countries in adopting new therapies, they are being reviewed by the FDA and may soon win approval.

## Further Exploration of the Role of Honey in Modern Medicine

Modern medicine has just begun to tap the therapeutic potential of honey. One day soon, its use in the fight against cataracts may be standard procedure. And its ability to promote wound healing and to kill bacteria already seems indisputable. Happily, scientists are continuing to investigate the curative powers of honey, including its anti-inflammatory properties, its ability to ease edema (swelling) and erythema (skin redness), its power as a promoter of collagen synthesis, tissue growth, and new skin formation, its potential as an antioxidant, its possible role in phagocytosis (when white blood cells attack invading pathogens), and much more.

It's interesting to note how many of the "newly discovered" medical properties of honey are not new at all. As we have seen, most of its therapeutic uses currently under investigation were known to physicians, shamans, and healers for many, many centuries. It seems that modern science has at last come to appreciate the value of a five-thousand-year-old folk remedy.

# Chapter 10

# How Sweet It Is: Cooking with Honey Through the Ages

HONEY CAN BE eaten dripping and gooey straight from the comb, drizzled on a slice of hot toast, or used as an ingredient in countless dishes, from simple, down-home cooking to the sumptuous fare served at the world's finest restaurants.

## The Golden Age of Honey

Metallic gold, it turns out, wasn't the only gold that caught the fancy of Midas, the legendary king with the golden touch, who ruled in western Turkey twenty-three hundred years ago. King Midas also had a taste for golden honey. When archaeologists analyzed food residues found in his tomb, they were able to re-create the menu of his burial banquet. Mourners assuaged their grief with appetizers of goat cheese, julienned cucumbers, olive paste, and dried figs. The main course was a stew of spicy lamb and lentils, followed by a caramelized honey and fennel tart. The beverages of choice were mead (honey wine), beer, and grape wine spiced with saffron. (A traveler in modern Turkey would find many of these dishes readily available at local restaurants.)

Roman cooks used honey not only as an ingredient in many desserts and sweet-and-sour entrées but also as a preservative for meat and fruit. Favorite dishes included cheese sweetened with honey, honey omelets, curds with honey, mushrooms sautéed in honey, and chilled white wine with honey added. The demand for honey was so great that most large Roman farms employed a full-time beekeeper, called an apiarus, to tend the hives.

# A Dish Fit for a King
# (Not to Mention a Queen
# and Her Favorite Poet)

Imagine that we've been invited to a sixteenth-century banquet at Hampton Court, a palace on the outskirts of London. Queen Elizabeth I is entertaining. The palace, a Renaissance masterpiece, has been home to a number of turbulent Tudor monarchs, including Elizabeth's parents, the unpredictable Henry VIII and his ill-fated consort Anne Boleyn. Most of the highborn guests have arrived with their retainers, who lurk vigilantly on the sidelines to make sure their masters and mistresses have all they need. Some members of the highest nobility, entangled as they are in dangerous political intrigue (for these are unsettled times), have brought along their personal tasters, to test the food for deadly ingredients that may have been secretly added to the recipes. Dogs are everywhere underfoot, gnawing the bones that, according to court etiquette, should be thrown on the floor rather than replaced on the serving tray from which they had been originally taken. Rising above the currents of boisterous conversation, the lilting strains of Renaissance music compete with clowns and acrobats leaping and tumbling through the air.

Now let's sample the rare and tempting dishes with which the long tables in the vast banquet hall are laden. This midsummer night's feast, fit for a powerful queen, might include succulent honey-glazed roasts turned slowly on a spit over a roaring fire, tiny game birds and acorn squash, lamb stew with prunes, cloves, mace, and saffron, dressed swan, pork with raisin and rosemary stuffing, salmon and figs baked in a pie, lavender biscuits, gooseberry tarts, gingerbread spiced with honey, and pears in a rich honey syrup, all washed down with large amounts of mead. The menu might also include exotic foods recently arrived in the Old World from the New World, such as tomatoes, maize, pineapple, chocolate, peanuts, hot peppers, and, just off the boat, turkey. Fortunately for Renaissance dentists in need of business, sugar from the West Indies is starting to make rapid inroads, replacing our beloved honey in many recipes and causing widespread tooth decay among the aristocracy, the only members of society who can afford it. Sugar, in fact, is the culprit that has blackened the teeth of the aging Virgin Queen. It is much more damaging to teeth than honey because it provides food for decay-causing microbes, while honey, with its antibiotic properties, kills many of those microbes.

The spices and honey used in many of the dishes add subtle complexities of flavor and aroma, but they also mask the stale, slightly rancid taste of some of the food. The fact is, fresh ingredients are not readily available in Tudor England, and refrigeration of modern home and supermarkets will not appear for hundreds of years.

As the evening wears on, the battalion of exhausted servers clears away the empty dishes and platters while the lute players retune their instruments and the minstrels prepare to sing. The queen is resplendent in her flaming red wig and stiffly brocaded gown.

If, after our Hampton Court banquet, we are invited to dine with the Ming emperor in China's Forbidden City, we might feast on grilled snake, bear claws, crispy king prawns served with honey-glazed walnuts, honey-glazed chicken wings (long before Buffalo, New York, got the idea), taro root with honey juice, steamed honey cakes, and, to aid the digestion, a swig of Canton ginger liqueur, rounded with honey.

Not to be outdone by his Chinese rival, Emperor Akbar of India now invites us to luncheon at the magnificent Red Fort in Delhi. Long before the Mughal conquest of India, ancient Sanskrit myths depicted the world as made up of seven concentric rings of land, separated by oceans of salt, jaggery (unrefined brown sugar), wine, ghee, milk, curds, and fresh water. All of these are still key ingredients in Indian cuisine, with the addition of honey, an important item in many Persian recipes brought to the subcontinent by the invading Mughals.

As our meal with the gracious Akbar begins, we find ourselves reclining on sumptuous pillows in a white marble pavilion inlaid with exquisite floral designs. Turbaned servants arrive bearing brass trays laden with exotic-looking dishes. After an appetizer of shrimp marinated in honey, vinegar, and spices, we turn our attention to fish baked with dill, fennel, and honey, fried dumplings dipped in honey sauce, and, for dessert, pastries stuffed with almond paste and honey and scented with rosewater, orange blossom water, and saffron.

As we continue our trip through culinary history, we might have occasion to sample a breakfast of yak yogurt with honey in Tibet, grapes dipped in honey in Armenia, Persian pastries made with rosewater and honey, and snow collected in the mountains of western Iran and flavored with honey and fruit juices, the refreshing forerunner of sorbet.

Next on our gastronomic itinerary is Turkey. Considered one of the three great cuisines of the world, along with French and Chinese, Turkish cooking is known for the uniqueness of its flavors and the universality of their appeal. Turkish cuisine has influenced cooking throughout Europe, the Middle East, and Africa. It originated in Central Asia, home of the first Turkish invaders of Anatolia, and evolved over the centuries as it came into contact with cuisines of the Mediterranean cultures that the Turks conquered.

In central Turkey, the ancient city of Konya made important contributions to the Turkish diet. During the twelfth century, Konya, capital of the Seljuk Empire (the first Turkish state in Anatolia), was a renowned cultural center that attracted scholars, mystics, and poets from throughout the world. It also attracted imaginative cooks who created many of the dishes, for which Konya has been famous ever since. This classic cuisine includes *böreks* (meat and vegetable dishes), tandir kebabs (a tandir is a clay oven buried in the earth), and halva, a sweet prepared with sesame oil, cereals, and honey.

When the Seljuk rulers were overthrown by the Ottomans in the late thirteenth century, the culinary arts in Turkey reached new heights. A visit to Topkapi Palace in Istanbul underscores the importance of fine dining to the Ottoman sultans. The huge palace kitchens were housed in several buildings under ten large domes. By the seventeenth century, some thirteen hundred workers were needed to staff the royal kitchens. Hundreds of cooks produced soups, pilafs, kebabs, fish, breads, pastries, candy, and halva to feed as many as ten thousand people a day.

The Arab historian Ibn Khaldun wrote, "The religion of the King, in time, becomes that of the people." The same clearly holds true for food. During the six-hundred-year reign of the Ottomans, the legacy of the imperial kitchens spread throughout their empire, influencing and refining countless regional dishes.

# What's Cooking: The Venerable Honey Cake

From the palaces of the Ottoman Empire, our journey now takes us to the castles and cathedrals of medieval Germany. By the time we reach Nuremberg, we may think we have had our fill of sweets, but we really must make room for *lebkuchen,* the classic honey cake taken to new heights by the bakers of this ancient walled city.

Of course, people had been making honey cakes for centuries. The Egyptians, believing honey to be a gift of the gods, hoped to acquire its life-giving properties by devouring it baked in cakes. Honey cakes were worn into battle as talismans and were buried with the pharaohs to accompany them to the next life. The *panis mellitus,* or honey bread, of the Romans was made of sesame flour soaked in honey after it had been cooked. Sliced and fried, it became *panis nauticus,* the sailor's biscuit. The Chinese are thought to have invented *mi-king,* a simple cake made of wheat flour and honey, around AD 900. Genghis Khan's horsemen carried *mi-king* in their saddlebags for a quick energy fix when they rode out to pillage and burn the Western world. During their conquests, the Mongols passed their taste for honey cake on to the Turks and Arabs. German pilgrims to the Holy Land acquired a passion for it and copied the recipe at home, where superstitious peasants believed it offered protection against evil spirits.

It was in a German monastery in the thirteenth

century that the ancient honey cake finally evolved into *lebkuchen*—a special gingerbread made with honey from the imperial forests near Nuremberg.

## Now You're Cooking!

After our long journey through the past, we're thoroughly homesick and ready for some real American cooking. The National Honey Board suggests you use honey to bring new life to many traditional favorites. Here are a few tips to give you a sense of the possibilities:

• To make your barbecue sauce more interesting, add a few spoonfuls of robust buckwheat, basswood, or sage honey.

• The next time you bake a batch of muffins, add orange blossom or clover honey to the batter.

• To glaze a roast chicken, you can't go wrong with sage or avocado honey.

• To liven up vanilla ice cream, let it soften, then spoon in some lavender or mixed wildflower honey.

• Try eucalyptus or sage honey in hot tea. On a torpid summer day, add clover, tupelo, or orange blossom honey to a glass of iced tea.

• Whip up some honey butter to melt on those piping hot rolls you set on the family dinner table.

# Honey Butter

*1 cup (2 sticks) unsalted butter, softened*
*1 cup (8 ounces) honey (use your favorite—*
*I like orange blossom)*
*½ teaspoon salt*

*Gently beat the ingredients together in a mixing bowl until smooth, then chill and enjoy.*

*Variations: Make herbed honey butter by mixing in 2 teaspoons fresh or dried rosemary, thyme, or lavender. For lemon honey butter, just add 2 teaspoons fresh lemon juice. I also like to add 1–2 teaspoons grated lemon zest.*

From honey butter, it's a short, easy step to . . .

# Honey Mustard

*¼ cup (2 ounces) mild honey, such as clover*
*¼ cup Dijon mustard*
*½ cup mayonnaise*

*Place the honey and mustard in a mixing bowl and whisk until smooth. Then whisk in the mayonnaise and chill in the refrigerator. When it's ready, you'll have a tangy dipping sauce, perfect for raw vegetables.*

*Variation: The honey mustard dipping sauce can be easily transformed into a zesty salad dressing with the addition of balsamic vinegar, a small amount of olive oil, black pepper, and maybe some chopped chives.*

## Orange Pineapple Honey Smoothie

1 or 2 cups diced canned pineapple (drained)
1 cup whole or 2% milk
1 cup plain yogurt
1/3 cup your favorite honey
4 tablespoons orange juice
2 teaspoons orange zest (from the orange rind)
10 ice cubes

*In a blender, combine all ingredients except the ice cubes and blend until perfectly smooth. Later, if desired, add ice cubes carefully, one at a time, until the drink is smooth.*

## Honey Rice Krispies Bar Treats

6 cups Rice Krispies
10-oz. package regular marshmallows
3 tablespoons butter or margarine
1/3 or 1/2 (even better) cup honey

Melt butter in a large saucepan over low heat. Add marshmallows a few at a time. Add honey and stir until all ingredients have melted. Remove from heat and set aside.

Add Rice Krispies and mix thoroughly.

Using a buttered spatula or waxed paper, press gooey mixture evenly into a 13 x 9 x 2–inch baking pan coated with nonstick cooking spray.

After cooling, about 15 minutes, cut into 2-inch squares. Enjoy your treat bars. They're best when served and eaten the same day you make them.

## Tips for Cooking with Honey

Here are some tips to keep in mind when cooking with honey. First, honey should always be stored at room temperature, never in the refrigerator or freezer. Keep it in your cupboard or pantry. It's natural for honey to change in character after a few months on the shelf. It may become cloudy or start to granulate (tiny crystals form, turning the liquid honey into a semisolid). Honey that has clouded or granulated can easily be restored to its original golden color and texture by applying a bit of heat. Be careful, though. If heated too much or too fast, honey can scorch or burn, losing its wonderful aroma. I usually warm it in a double boiler, submerging half to three-quarters of the uncovered jar in water. Stir the honey frequently, and the cloudiness and crystals will disappear.

If you are in a hurry, uncap the honey jar and place it in a microwave oven. Make sure the setting is on low or medium at most. Stop and check the honey every thirty seconds or so. Whatever you do, don't boil it. You want it just hot enough to dissolve the crystals.

Cooking with honey can be a sticky business. To avoid making a mess, try a traditional wooden or plastic honey dipper. It looks like a spoon but has little flanges to prevent the honey from dripping (see what one looks like on the cover of this book). Better yet, store your honey in a plastic squeeze container. There's almost no dripping with this method. Now you know why honey bears are such cherished honey containers at the market.

Measuring honey in a glass or plastic measuring cup can present a problem. To make sure the honey pours out of the cup easily, apply vegetable oil to the inside of the cup. If your recipe calls for both oil and honey, just measure the oil first and then measure the honey in the same cup. Leaving the honey out at room temperature or gently warming it makes it easier to pour and mix with other ingredients.

Cooking with honey can make a big difference in your enjoyment of many foods. It adds to and brings out the flavor of the other ingredients it's mixed with. It keeps breads and cakes moist and flavorful and extends their normal shelf life. (That's because honey attracts and absorbs moisture, but you already knew that.) Honey can also add a rich, golden color to the crusts of pies and tarts.

Sugar and honey aren't created equal. Honey is 80 percent sugar and 20 percent water, while cane and beet sugars are 100 percent sugar. When substituting honey for table sugar in any recipe, you need to make a few small but important changes. As a general rule, when replacing sugar with honey, use half the amount of honey as sugar called for in the recipe. Because honey is 20 percent water, you also need to reduce the amount of liquid (water, milk, fruit juice, etc.) in your recipe by one tablespoon for each four tablespoons of honey. It's also a good idea to add one-half teaspoon of baking soda to the recipe for each cup of honey used. When baking your sweet sensation, remember to reduce the oven temperature by 25°F. This will prevent overbrowning or burning.

## Infant Botulism and Honey

I WOULD BE remiss if I failed to warn readers about the risk of giving honey to infants, either right out of the jar or added to food and beverages. The fact is, babies under twelve months of age should never be given honey. This is because, in rare cases, honey has been found to contain spores of *Clostridium botulinum*, the rod-shaped bacterium that causes botulism. Infants are susceptible to this form of poisoning, though it is not a problem after their first birthday. The number of infant botulism cases reported in the United States in a typical year is about one hundred, an extremely low incidence. Some doctors believe that honey fed to babies may be related to cases of sudden infant death syndrome (SIDS, or crib death).

Of course, honey is completely safe for older children and adults, a healthy food to be enjoyed frequently in all its delicious varieties.

# Afterword

Bees are important. In the United States there are 4,000 different kinds of bees. This includes the familiar European honey bee, charismatic black-and-yellow bumble bees, giant black carpenter bees, and less familiar kinds: sweat bees, mining bees, cuckoo bees, leafcutters and masons, squash and gourd bees. They come in all colors, shapes, and sizes. Some are furry all over like miniature flying "teddy bears," while others have smooth and shiny polished metallic bodies and legs that glisten in colors of green, blue, and copper. Some are larger than the world's smallest hummingbird, while the tiniest are smaller than fruit flies, tiny specks with four wings. Most don't make honey and wax or live together in nests as family groups headed by a queen mother. Almost all are females leading solitary lives (think of them as single moms with families to feed) excavating underground burrows or living in abandoned beetle burrows in the wood of dead trees or branches. In Appendix 1, you will learn about the lives of the less familiar bees, the masons, leafcutters, diggers, and carpenters.

All bees visit flowers for pollen and nectar. Even

parasitic bees (called cuckoos) have to visit flowers to collect nectar as food and flight fuel. Because most have branched, almost featherlike hairs, pollen grains from flowers easily attach to their bodies. Bees are neat and tidy, but they can't groom off all the pollen to take back home as food. A scant dusting of pollen is left in hideaway spots on their bodies. This is what makes them champion pollinators. Unknowingly, as the bees forage for food, they are dusting new flowers with pollen, pollinating the blossoms. Later, this leads to fertilization and creates seeds inside fruits. Bees, other insects, and animal pollinators are responsible for helping produce about 35 percent of our global food supply; every third bite of food we eat, we should thank a pollinator. Most of the calories needed to feed the earth's nearly seven billion human beings come from wind-pollinated plants (rice, corn, wheat, barley, millet). And bees pollinate most of the tasty fruits and vegetables that we like to eat. These fruits put vital nutrients and vitamins into our diet, keeping us healthy and happy.

Bees do more for us and for other animals and plants than pollinate flowers. There are many "ecosystem services" they do as they go about making a living. Because most bees are ground-nesting, the burrows they dig are channels that get water into the soil. So we can think of bees as being like earthworms. And since they carry nitrogen-rich pollen grains into the soil, which are eaten by their larvae and defecated belowground, they are important in fertilizing the soil and aiding soil formation.

146

Bees and other pollinators are also food themselves for mice, skunks, bears, lizards, birds, and bats. And, of course, the honey makers make beeswax that we use for candles as well as the oozing golden amber treasure we know as honey.

Lately, however, bees and other pollinators need our help. Habitat loss, invasive animals and plants, diseases, pollution, insecticides, and herbicides have all reduced the populations of managed and native bees. You may have heard about Colony Collapse Disorder (CCD), which has killed many thousands of honey bee colonies in the United States and around the world. We still don't know what caused this calamity for crop pollination. Is CCD caused by environmental stress, diseases, or pesticides? It is likely not caused by a single factor. We simply don't know. Similarly, some of our native bees, the colorful bumble bees that pollinate tomatoes, blueberries, cranberries, and many wild plants, are now threatened. Many bumble bees that were common twenty years ago can no longer be found where they once lived. Scientists believe that one or more imported European bee diseases are spreading through their populations, killing off the bee colonies.

Everything isn't all doom and gloom. You and your family, friends, and neighbors can do simple yet vitally important things to help protect bees, other pollinators, and flowering plants. One easy thing to do is to plant a pollinator garden, or even just a few flowers in a pot or window box. If you use native plants, these will grow easily since they are accustomed to local climate and soils. They also don't need much extra TLC to grow and prosper. If you buy plants from a nursery, ask for old-fashioned heirloom varieties. These plants have the full complement of tasty nectar and pollen that bees and other pollinators need. Avoid modern hybrid flowers, which often lack nectar and pollen. Plant lots of flowers if you can, in clumps of four or more plants. Try to have some blooms in your yard from spring to fall. Avoid using insecticides if possible, or spray at night when bees aren't active. Remember, caterpillars turn into butterflies and moths, which are pollinators. Plant extra for the caterpillars, and learn to appreciate and tolerate a few bug holes in leaves.

Some of the most fun you can have is to become a bee watcher. Pollinators make great pets because they feed and care for themselves. You can watch butterflies with close-focusing binoculars. Come nose to nose with bees on flowers and learn about pollination. By drilling holes in scrap lumber, you can create a "bee condo," a home for leafcutter and mason bees, which are wonderful garden and fruit tree pollinators. Become a citizen or student scientist and become involved with nature study. You can join in butterfly counts with the North American Butterfly Association (www.naba.org), and you can learn about bees and other pollinators by becoming a partner of the Pollinator Partnership (www.pollinator.org) or becoming a member of the Xerces Society (www.xerces.org). Why not plant some sunflowers and report what bees you see visiting them to Gretchen, online at the Great Sunflower Project (www.greatsunflower.org)? These are just a few of the ways you and your family can make a difference for pollinators and enrich your own lives at the same time.

## Steve's Top Ten Things You and Your Family Can Do to Help Bees

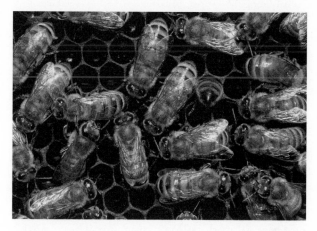

1. Plant lots of tasty wildflowers, using native flowers or heirloom varieties and avoiding modern hybrids. Consider getting rid of your lawn or reducing its size. Lawns are bee deserts.

2. Plant flowers in clumps of four or more plants. Plant various kinds of flowers that will bloom at different times, from spring to fall. Plant a pollinator meadow if you have the space.

3. Try not to use insecticides or herbicides. If you have to use them, follow label instructions and wear protective clothing and take all other recommended precautions.

4. Leave dead trees and branches alone. Bees and wasps live in abandoned beetle holes or dig their own nests like the carpenter bees.

5. Use scrap lumber to drill holes and make a bee condominium. Nail it under the eaves of your house and patio to create new nesting habitat for leafcutter and mason bees.

6. Leave some bare ground around. Native bees need this for nesting. Covering everything with mulch eliminates places where bees can live.

7. Create a muddy spot where mason bees can come and collect mud for their nests. Even a plastic one-gallon milk jug with a pin-hole in the bottom will help.

8. Go to your library or your local bookstore or go online and read about bees and other pollinators. Visit www.pollinator.org.

9. Become a bee watcher! Keep a notebook, use a close-focusing point-and-shoot camera to take your own bee and flower photographs. Join an organization like the ones mentioned

earlier, and visit their Web sites for the latest pollinator news.

10. Tell your family about organic farmers and how they are helping bees and other wildlife. Plan a visit to a local farmers' market. Buy local honey! Try a natural, comb honey for a real taste sensation. Visit the Pollinator Partnership Web site (www.pollinator.org).

# Acknowledgments

I have fond memories of observing honey bees and native bees through fields of spring wildflowers with my daughters, Marlyse and Melissa, when they were teenagers. For teaching me the ways of bees, I gratefully thank: Robbin Thorp, Paul Cooper, Makhdzir bin Mardan, Thomas Seeley, Hayward Spangler, Justin Schmidt, Steven Thoenes, and Adrian Wenner. For funding bee projects, I gratefully acknowledge the Wallace Family Foundations and the Geraldine R. Dodge Foundation, Paul and Eileen Growald, and Laurie Davies Adams of the Pollinator Partnership. Thanks to Joshua Mailman, Robert E. Turner and his sons, Rhett and Beau, for their efforts on behalf of pollinators, and to Mike Philips of the Turner Endangered Species Fund. Special thanks to Melanie Adcock of the CS Fund and "house-boatin'" Diana Cohn of the Panta Rhea Foundation for funding research and educational outreach in Quintana Roo, Mexico.

I sincerely thank many friends for spirited discussions about bees, flowers, and honey: Beth Armbrust, Patricia

Cowan, Alison Deming, Arthur Donovan, Mark Dimmitt, Matilda Essig, Richard Felger, Steve Hopp, Barbara Kingsolver, Kimberly Larson, Margrit McIntosh, Paul Mirocha, Gary Nabhan, Shelly Pope, Sarah Richardson, Hayward Spangler, Barbara Terkanian, Cristina Trimble, and Michael Wilson. A special thanks to Kimberly Larson, for hosting the best-ever honey-tasting party, and to her children, Taylor, Lauren, and Reed, for helping create and kid test "teen friendly" honey recipes. I thank Dr. Richard Jones and the late Dr. Eva Crane of the International Bee Research Association in Cardiff, Wales, for permission to reprint antiquarian art. And thanks to the National Honey Board for permission to reprint their recipes.

I thank the staff of the University of Arizona libraries for helping me track down obscure references. I thank Christine Cairns, Harriet J. de Jong, Julio Lopez, and Gabrielle Vail for their writings about Mayan meliponiculture and endangered traditions. And I thank Troy Sagrillo for providing unpublished photographs of Egyptian tomb and temple art.

A special thanks to my literary agent, and manuka honey devotee, Judith Riven of New York City. Thank you, Judith! To Banning Repplier, who was coauthor for my adult title, I extend warmest thanks for climbing aboard the honey wagon. To Beth Rashbaum at Bantam Books, Beverly Horowitz and Rebecca Gudelis at Delacorte Press, and copy editor Joy Simpkins, I extend sincerest thanks for editorial suggestions, wordsmithing, and shepherding the book from proposal to publication. To Paul Mirocha, my Tucson friend and fellow traveler to Malaysian honey hunts, my sincere thanks for some of the interior art. Paul is the king bee of pollinator art, and a fine mandolin picker.

# Appendix 1
# Bees of the World:
# A Remarkable Beestiary

Bees differ from wasps and ants, their relatives, by certain physical and behavioral characteristics. They are covered with branched hairs (almost like feathers), all the better to hold pollen. They have constricted waists, which gives them flexibility when turning in their narrow burrows. More than 100 million years ago, during the rise of flowering plants, the first bees evolved from predatory hunting wasps. Although some of the world's bees are partial meat eaters, the vast majority are content to be vegan, dining on sweet hoards of nectar, pollen, and honey.

Most bees are solitary creatures. They don't live as complex societies inside large nests and they do not store honey. Instead, they do their own thing. Each female is completely self-reliant, excavating her own nest and foraging for her own nectar and pollen, which she eats on the spot or brings back to her nest for her developing larvae to consume right away. The exceptions are European honey bees (*Apis mellifera*) and a few others, such as bumble bees (genus *Bombus*) and the stingless bees of the Mayan homelands (*Melipona* and *Trigona*). They collect nectar and store the honey produced. Modern bee-keepers aid this natural hoarding tendency by giving honey bees more room in their hives than they actually need, encouraging them to produce the surplus that eventually finds its way to our tables.

Scientists who study bees are called mellitologists (apiculturists are experts who study only honey bees). These experts are confronted with a huge task. *The Bees of the World,* a 913-page book published in 2002 by Charles Michener, recognizes seven families and 425 genera of bees worldwide. Within the genera, twenty thousand bee species have been described so far. Estimates of how many species are really out there, including those yet to be discovered and formally named, range from twenty-five thousand to thirty thousand. There are about four thousand bee species (in one hundred genera) in the United States, seven thousand in South America, roughly four thousand in Africa, and three thousand in Australia.

Given these numbers, it is not surprising that the world is literally full of bees—bees of all imaginable sizes, shapes, colors, and lifestyles and living in all sorts of habitats. From sea level to altitudes of over fourteen thousand feet, bees have invaded and colonized every part of the planet that offers flowering plants and places to nest. Only Antarctica and the northernmost islands of the Canadian tundra are without bees.

# True Honey Bees (the genus *Apis*)

The first known honey bees date back forty million years to the Eocene Age. Specimens of later honey bees are found preserved in fossilized amber from Germany, Poland, and Scandinavia. But most honey bees appear to have evolved in tropical lowland forests, where they are abundant today. The familiar European honey bee (*Apis mellifera*) is believed to have originated in the African tropics, then migrated westward into Asia, and northward into colder European climates. Until modern times, *Apis mellifera* was not found anywhere in the Western Hemisphere, Australia, or the remote Pacific islands, but European settlers imported them for commercial purposes, so they are now global citizens. In the United States, the honey bees that buzz through our gardens are the result of planned and unplanned introductions to our shores. Many are the descendants of forebears who were deliberately brought to Mexico by Spanish beekeepers; others came aboard English ships laden with colonists and their homesteading supplies, bound for Jamestown and Plymouth Rock a little more than four hundred years ago.

Depending on which bee scientist you talk to, there are seven to nine or even eleven species of true honey bees, all members of the genus *Apis*. (In this book, I have considered the genus *Apis* to include eleven living species.) The first scientist to recognize, classify, and name honey bees was the Swedish naturalist Carl von Linné, better known as Linnaeus. He described the genus *Apis* in the year 1758. The actual specimen described by Linnaeus

246 years ago can be seen today in the Natural History Museum, London, skewered on a pin above a faded label written in Linnaeus's own hand. Having miraculously survived fires, floods, world wars, carpet beetles, mold, and human negligence, it remains the gold standard—the prototypical honey bee specimen to which all others of its kind are compared.

The eleven honey bee species belong to three subgroups: giant honey bees (subgenus *Megapis*), dwarf honey bees (subgenus *Micrapis*), and European and related honey bees (subgenus *Apis*). Most of the bees in these subgroups originated in the tropical regions of Asia. Only *Apis mellifera* and *Apis cerana* have been "domesticated" and kept in man-made hives, although all have been robbed of their honey by human and animal predators. Actually, we just give honey bees comfy boxes to live inside; we really haven't selected (bred) them like we've done with farm animals, dogs, and cats.

There are two main species of giant honey bee in the subgenus *Megapis: Apis laboriosa* and *Apis dorsata. Apis laboriosa,* the world's largest honey bee, nest on remote cliffsides in the Himalayas of Nepal. The worker bees are up to .75 inch long, and their colonies number from twenty thousand to sixty thousand, all living in massive, half-moon-shaped combs. *Apis dorsata* nest high in trees of tropical rain forests such as those in Malaysia, Thailand, Vietnam, and Borneo, although some have made the move to man-made structures—such as tall buildings and water towers—in those regions.

Colonies of *Apis dorsata* must always be approached with extreme caution. People walking below their nests can trigger a massive and potentially life-threatening attack. *Apis dorsata* form living blankets covering both sides of combs that can be up to five feet across. Honey is stored in the upper part of the nest, where it attaches to the underside of massive branches. Favorite trees, such as the towering tualang tree of Malaysia, host dozens of colonies. Individual tualang trees are known to have as many as 120 distinct nests among their branches!

Although the extreme height of tualang trees would seem to entirely protect the bees, the lowland Asian rain forests are home to the giant sloth or honey bear. These animals come well equipped for nest robbing, with strong claws for climbing and a foot-long tongue, ideal for lapping up sweet honey and eating bee brood. Another worry for the bees are honey buzzards, which circle above, waiting for an opportunity to plunder the nests. And then there are human honey hunters, including Pak Teh and his clan.

A still mysterious aspect of the giant honey bee is that they migrate great distances, following the bloom in search of nectar flows. In the Pedu Lake region of Malaysia, the first *Apis dorsata* return to their favorite tualang trees in November or December from unknown places. They begin to make wax to build the combs where they will store honey and rear the brood. In late February or March, the colonies begin to leave, one by one, to once again begin their mysterious migrations.

The spectacle and roar of these huge colonies leaving their giant combs is a sight I will never forget. Sailors and ship captains have reported seeing migrating colonies crossing the Strait of Malacca from the Malaysian mainland to the island of Sumatra.

There are two dwarf honey bees (subgenus *Micrapis*), one of which, *Apis florea*, is only .35 inch long—the length of a European honey bee's abdomen. Unlike the European honey bee (*Apis mellifera*), these bees don't build multiple combs or nest in dark cavities. They build a single comb, attached to the branches of plants. The surfaces of their delicate combs are protected from the rain, sun, and wind by a living blanket of bees. *Apis florea* is rarely seen because they hide their colonies, about six thousand bees, in dense foliage.

*Apis florea* are gentle bees, of small size and having a small stinger. They are barely able to sting. Their worker bees act as security guards, ready to chase away attackers, including weaver ants. They collect sticky plant resins and apply these to the branch supports to keep ants from attacking. When under attack by a mammal or bird, these gentle bees abandon their nests. *Apis florea* store the smallest amount of honey (about one quart per year). Even so, these tiny bee nests have been plundered for millennia by humans and other honey-loving animals. In food markets in Bangkok, Thailand, you can find *Apis florea* nests for sale, still attached to their branches. These nests are gathered from the wild because *Apis florea* are not managed by beekeepers. Their honey provides a special treat for many Thai families and is greatly prized.

## The Other Bees: From the World's Smallest Bee to the World's Largest

The world's smallest bee, *Perdita minima,* occurs in my front yard. Its body is only .078 inch long, small enough to crawl through the fine mesh of most insect nets. I locate them by the faint shadows they cast on bare earth and sidewalks. They visit and pollinate tiny white flowers of the native mat euphorbias. These weedy plants poke up through cracks in sidewalks around town and in the desert. A stingless bee from the Amazon may be even slightly smaller than *Perdita minima*. One can almost imagine these bees struggling with a single pollen grain to bring home to feed the kids.

The world's largest bee, *Chalicodoma pluto,* is 1.6 inches long and shares its nest with tree-loving termites in the Moluccas, the famed Spice Islands. It was first collected in the Moluccan rain forest in 1859 by Alfred Russel Wallace, the cofounder of the theory of evolution. The specimen is in the Natural History Museum in London. This elusive bee was lost to science until rediscovered in the 1970s by Adam Messer, then a graduate student at the University of Georgia. Little is known about *Chalicodoma pluto* other than its belonging to the leafcutter family of bees, which cut leaves to use in their nests. Other bees of this family have likely visited rosebushes in your garden, leaving behind visible traces of their handiwork.

More common are the gentle giants known as carpenter bees (genus *Xylocopa*). Along with bumble bee queens and orchid bees, these are the largest bees in North America. Carpenter bees excavate galleries in dead wood with their powerful jaws and reuse the galleries year after year.

## Cuckoo Bees: Bees in Wolves' Clothing

These bees are colorful and sleek, with little or no fur. That's because, due to their stealthy lifestyle, they don't need fuzz because they don't transport pollen. Instead of making an "honest living," building their own nests and collecting food, they prey on others. Scientists call them cleptoparasites; we call them cuckoo bees, for like cowbirds, they sneak their eggs into another nest, usually when the owner is out shopping. The parasite's egg hatches first and the young cuckoo larva kills and eats the host bee eggs. Next, it gorges on pollen and nectar the host mother has gathered for her young. The cuckoo bees then emerge, mate, and seek out new host nests to begin the cycle all over again. It may not seem fair, but evolution has helped make cuckoo bees a successful alternate life strategy.

## Polyester Bees

The Colletidae family of bees line their underground tunnels and cells with a clear, durable material similar to cellophane. This ensures that the level of humidity in the brood cells will be just right for the eggs and developing larvae. Bees are masterful chemists, and colletids are no exception. Some of them produce compounds known as macrocyclic lactones. You might know these substances by their other name, polyester. Colletid bees may not wear miniature retro-style leisure suits of the 1970s, but they are polyester-making bees nonetheless.

## Mining Bees

Each spring, university entomology departments are besieged with phone calls from homeowners wanting to know who or what is responsible for the little mounds of soil mysteriously appearing on their lawns. The culprits, it turns out, are mining bees, which dig thin tunnels below the ground in which to shape their nests and raise their larvae. The architecture of these nests can be elaborate. They may contain just one cell or dozens.

## Mason Bees

Not with trowels but with mandibles and specialized "tools" on their legs, many bees are specialists at collecting and using mud, resins, chewed leaves, and pebbles to shape these found materials into snug, waterproof nurseries, or brood cells, for their developing larvae. Often, these bees don't dig their own nests but simply find and then "redecorate" abandoned beetle burrows with their own cell partitions and end plugs. The blue orchard bee (*Osmia lignaria*) is one kind of mason, common to the Pacific Northwest states. It is a champion pollinator of fruit trees, especially apple, plum, and sweet cherry—more efficient, in fact, than the industrious honey bee. These bees are now being tested as almond pollinators. Live blue orchard bees can be ordered from dealers or purchased in some home garden centers. Commercial bee houses are available for these helpful pollinators, or you can drill holes in scrap lumber to make your own bee condos.

## Sweating for Sweat Bees

Ever been gardening and had a small black or metallic greenish-brown bee land on your forearm and lick beads of perspiration? If so, you've encountered a sweat bee of the large Halictidae family. This family includes solitary species as well as primitively social kinds that have worker castes and queens. These largely ground-nesting bees pollinate many kinds of flowers and tend to be generalists. One kind of sweat bee (*Halictus ligatus*) even nests underneath asphalt parking lots. That's one tough little bee.

## Other Honey Makers: Ants and Wasps with a Sweet Tooth

Some ant and wasp species act like the bees, making and storing honey in their nests. The so-called honeypot ants (*Myrmecocystus* spp.) of the American deserts collect nectar and honeydew from scale insects, then stockpile the liquid honey in an unusual way. Certain worker ants, called repletes, actually become living honey jars! They greet returning foragers and tap out a message in ant Morse code. This causes the foragers to regurgitate honey to them. The repletes swell with the transferred honey until they are round and grotesquely distended. These living tankards hang patiently from the roof of their underground nest until tapped into service by their hungry sisters.

I once had an interesting encounter with honeypot ants near the Arizona–New Mexico border. I was staying at the Southwestern Research Station, operated by the American Museum of Natural History, while studying buzz-pollinating bees that visit deadly nightshade blossoms. One morning, on my way to the nightshade patch, I stopped alongside an excavation in progress and met Harvard myrmecologist Gary Alpert for the first time.

Using a John Deere backhoe borrowed from a kindly cattle rancher, Gary was excavating a honeypot nest—a big job. These ants often burrow fifteen feet or more into the rocky desert soil. He reached the bottom of the nest and broke into galleries containing dozens of ant repletes. When Gary popped one of the ants into his mouth, I was surprised, but then did the same. After all, Aborigines in Australia have dined for centuries on sweet repletes, so why couldn't I? I held the struggling ant by its head and legs, popped its ready-to-burst abdomen with my teeth. I felt, then tasted, the acidic honey hit my tongue. Acidic (perhaps due to formic acid), yes, but delicious. As I tossed the emptied ant husk away and grabbed another, I wondered what flowers or scale insects the ants had visited and how far they had traveled to collect the honey for our impromptu desert feast.

A few tropical wasps (genus *Brachygastra*) are also in the honey business. They live in Texas, Mexico, and Central America in delicate yet durable paper nests. Their open-faced, upside-down paper combs, enclosed in a protective outer sheath, are filled with dark honey, almost molasses-like in consistency and taste. One kind, *Brachygastra mellifica,* from the forests of Guanacaste province in Costa Rica, lives in nests with tens of thousands of sisters and their queen. They defend their honey-laden nests fiercely when humans get too close. Interestingly, like honey bees and certain harvester ants, they are a select group of hymenopterans with barbed stingers. Having a barbed stinger has its drawbacks, since the stinging individual loses its life along with its stinger. As with all bees, ants, and wasps, it is only the females that sting. Males have no stingers. Some tribes in northwest Mexico seek out *Brachygastra* wasps and make off with their honeycombs. They chew the combs, spitting out the paper wads, then go back for more—a real treat in a region offering few natural sweets.

# APPENDIX 2
# Other Products of the Hive

When someone mentions bees, our thoughts naturally turn to honey, but there are other important substances collected or produced by honey bees and stored away in their nests. This section is about those products, which we'll examine a bit closer.

## Beeswax

Beeswax is the concrete, steel, and glass of the bee nest. With it, the bees construct walls, ceilings, honey and pollen pantries, nurseries for their brood, and even dance floors to waggle around on.

In the first scientific study of the efficiency of beeswax production, Justin Schmidt and I found that beeswax is biochemically expensive to produce. We fed mixtures of 50 percent sugar and 50 percent water to caged honey bees of wax-producing age. Hanging in chains of interlocked legs, the young bees guzzled sugar water and began secreting wax from four paired glands under their abdomens. We measured their wax output by weighing the beautiful white combs during the course of our experiment. Based on these measurements, we found that bees must eat, then metabolize, twenty pounds of honey to make every pound of wax, turning simple sugars into the complex lipids. At this rate, it could take eighty thousand or more worker bees to produce sixty pounds of fresh wax.

If you study a worker bee with a microscope or hand lens, you'll see the eight wax glands on the underside of her abdomen. The outer surface of the glands are flat, shiny oval areas known as wax mirrors. Wax is secreted as a clear liquid that floods the wax mirrors, then quickly hardens into scales and turns translucent white. It takes 910,000 of the tiny scales to make 2.2 pounds of beeswax. The wax-making bee or one of her sisters collects the wax scales and takes them to the comb construction site. To make the walls of the cells and the caps that seal them, the bees manipulate the scales with their mandibles and add enzymes and saliva to the mix. The now pliable wax is fashioned, without a blueprint, into the individual cells, which are joined side to side and end to end to form the double-sided combs. Remember, we mentioned earlier how the hexagonal shapes and 120-degree angles may actually take on that form due to properties of the wax itself. Each waxen cell wall is only 1/350 inch thick—thin but strong enough to resist deformation. The only threat to the wax structures is heat. On hot days, forager bees scatter tiny water droplets on the combs and fan their wings like crazy to prevent a core meltdown.

# The Uses of Beeswax Outside the Hive

The ancient Persians and Assyrians used beeswax to embalm their dead. In Egypt, cosmetologists added beeswax to facial creams, lip balms (just like the lip balm from Burt's Bees), nail polishes, and hair dressings. Egyptian artists mixed ground pigments into molten beeswax to make a special kind of paint called encaustic. This was ideal for portraying figures on flat slabs of stone. Among the Maya, Inca, Babylonians, and others, beeswax was used in the process of lost-wax casting, especially for fine silver and gold jewelry. I've even tried the lost-wax process and have some new "bee bling," a silver neck pendant in the size and shape of an Arizona carpenter bee pupa. Greek doctors prescribed beeswax, liquefied and diluted with water, to soothe mucous membranes and curb dysentery and diarrhea. Medieval Europeans sealed important documents with beeswax to guard the intrigues they were forever plotting. Popes and kings and other aristocrats used special sealing rings to authenticate their letters and special documents.

One of the most enduring uses of beeswax is the production of candles. Beeswax candles are famous for their pleasant fragrance and bright, clean-burning flames. Beeswax was probably the first wax used in candle making and was far superior to the smoky, foul-smelling candles the poor made from rendered beef tallow. Today, paraffin, a by-product of petroleum refining, is used to make cheaper candles.

Probably the largest consumer of beeswax candles is

the Catholic Church. In the past, candles made of beeswax secreted by "virgin bees" symbolized the virgin birth of Christ, his "spotless" body, and the pure light of the world. The wick represented Christ's soul, the flame his divine and human nature. The burning of sacramental candles reminded the faithful of Christ's death on the cross. Beeswax candles are still blessed by Catholic priests on Candlemas Day, celebrated each year on February 2. By papal decree, church candles must be at least 51 percent beeswax. Originally, the Church required that sanctuary candles be 100 percent beeswax.

But candles are only part of the story. Today, hundreds of commercial products are made with beeswax, from cosmetics, skin ointments, stick colognes, and antiperspirants to shoe polishes, furniture and automobile waxes, industrial lubricants, and various anticorrosion coatings.

Thanks to all these uses, beeswax is big business. The Food and Agriculture Organization of the United Nations estimates the world production of beeswax at 44 million pounds a year, worth about 25 million U.S. dollars.

## Bee Pollen

Bees don't make pollen; they collect it from flowers, then turn it into bee bread (pollen that has been inoculated with yogurtlike bacteria), which they store in uncapped brood comb cells until used.

The pollen grains are produced inside the anthers of flowering plants. Within the tough outer shell of each grain are the plant's sex cells, similar to sperm cells in animals. These cells are suspended in an inner goo, called cytoplasm, rich in proteins, nitrogen, nucleic acids, amino acids, lipids, antioxidants, and other nutrients. This is what makes pollen perfect bee food. Nectar and honey contribute energizing sugars to the bee diet.

Each honey bee colony collects an average of twenty to forty pounds of pollen every year. Foragers then add regurgitated nectar and saliva to the pollen grains they collect from flowers until they attain a Play-Doh-like consistency easily transported in their hind leg "pollen baskets." Back at the nest, pollen foragers look for empty cells close to the active brood cells on a brood comb. They then back in and rub their hind legs together, dislodging the pollen pellets. Other foragers add their pellets until the cell is about half full. House bees tamp and poke the pollen, adding honey, saliva, and other secretions, and it is gradually transformed into the amazing substance known as bee bread.

## Pollen for People?

Attractively packaged, bee pollen is marketed as a miracle food for humans. But the fact remains, none of its reputed health claims have been verified in controlled clinical trials. Though high in proteins, lipids, minerals, antioxidants, and vitamins, these nutrients can be obtained in other, more easily digested foods at considerably lower cost.

Some people experience serious side effects when they

eat bee pollen. Major adverse reactions can include stomach pain and diarrhea, reported by up to 33 percent of individuals in some studies. Irritation or itching of the mouth and throat are also sometimes reported. So, be completely safe and eat it very cautiously. Or, better yet, leave bee pollen to the bees and enjoy their honey instead. I do encourage everyone to explore the amazing diversity of pollen shapes, sizes, and textures by looking at pollen grains under a microscope.

## Propolis (It's Bee Glue)

Beekeepers may use Elmer's Glue-All to strengthen the joints of their wooden Langstroth frames, but honey bees have a special glue all their own. Beekeepers call the brown, yellow, or green substance propolis, and sometimes complain because it sticks frames and hive parts together and makes inspecting hives more difficult.

Honey bees collect propolis from the resins, saps, and gums that they scrape from the stems and leaves of flowering plants. Plants have a long history of producing such chemical compounds for their constant struggle with fungi, bacteria, and herbivorous animals. Some of the chemicals are poisonous, such as the glycosides in milkweed sap, while others provide sticky physical barriers that stop predators in their tracks.

Bees usually keep plenty of propolis on hand. They use it for caulking, sealing, strengthening, lining, and varnishing just about everything in the nest. When they construct nests in rock cavities, they "paint" a ring of propolis around the colony to keep marauding ants away. Ants and bees are age-old enemies.

## Propolis for People?

Propolis had several components that can make it an effective therapeutic agent for humans. It contains flavones pinocembrin, galangin, and caffeic and ferulic acids, all active against many bacteria and may be useful in healing wounds. It also contains quercetin, a flavone that has both antiviral and capillary-strengthening properties. Some of the flavonoids in propolis are capable of scavenging free radicals and protecting lipids and may even inhibit melanoma and carcinoma in certain tumor cells.

Though propolis was used medicinally by the ancients, it had fallen out of favor until a few decades ago. Today, it is used for alleviating gum disease and is sometimes added to toothpastes. It does not seem to be toxic to humans, even when taken in moderate doses, though it can cause contact dermatitis in some people.

Unfortunately, there have been no clinical studies to test the medical benefits of propolis other than in oral hygiene. That's too bad, because it's an area worth investigating.

## Royal Jelly

You may have seen small bottles of royal jelly glistening on department store shelves in cosmetics departments. You may have wondered what it is and gasped at its high price. Royal jelly is a product of the bees, secreted by hypopharyngeal glands within the heads of young worker bees. All bee larvae are fed royal jelly the first three days of their larval lives. From the fourth day on, drone and worker larvae are fed pollen and honey instead, while larvae destined to become queens continue to dine solely on royal jelly. The development of a fertilized bee egg into a queen or worker is just a matter of differing nutrition. Scientists still don't quite understand how this happens, but it is an area of active research. Royal jelly is 67 percent water, 11 percent sugar, 5 percent fatty acids, and 13 percent crude protein. It also contains cholesterol and other sterols as well as zinc, iron, copper, manganese, and high levels of the B vitamins.

## A Lucrative Skin Care Business

A number of health and cosmetic properties have been attributed to royal jelly over the years, but none has been confirmed by controlled scientific clinical studies. Other than a few exotic fatty acids, there is nothing special or magical in royal jelly, and nothing you can't get from other, much less expensive foods. Claims of tissue repair, moisturizing properties, and other dermatological benefits need to be clinically tested to be deemed credible.

Royal jelly is big business across Asia, where manufacturers do their best to hype the royal connection, the mystique of the queen bee, and its touted antiaging powers. Most of the world's supply comes from rural Chinese factories, where women painstakingly extract minute amounts from queen cells housed in special brood frames. China produces more than eight hundred tons of royal jelly each year! While its benefits, even in cosmetics, are questionable, royal jelly, at six dollars and more per ounce, commands regal prices. Once again, glamour wins out over scientific fact and possibly common sense and reason.

## Bee Venom

Bee venom is a complex liquid secreted in the honey bee's poison gland and delivered through the aculeus, a stinger like a hypodermic needle. Only females have stingers, leaving the unarmed males dependent on their sisters for protection. Millions of years ago, the stinger started out as a tool for inserting eggs into plant stems or animal prey so developing larvae could feed inside in relative safety. Later, venom took on a defensive role to fend off attackers, especially mammals and birds. Contrary to popular belief, honey bees that lose their stingers don't die instantly. It's true they are partially eviscerated when the stinger is pulled out, but they may live for several hours. Beekeepers are familiar with these "stung-out," kamikaze-like bees. They've lost their barbed weapon and chemical ammunition, but nature has given them an edge in psychological warfare against much larger enemies. People are easily harassed by the relentless dive-bombing of harmless, stung-out bees, desperately swatting at them and often doing more damage to themselves than to the bees.

Venom is a bitter-tasting soup of proteins, peptides, and other biochemicals. Melittin, the main peptide, is the one that causes pain at the sting site. As a general rule, humans can survive if they receive six or fewer bee stings per pound of body weight. They have a 50 percent chance of survival at eight stings per pound and will probably die at ten stings per pound. This means that the average healthy adult male or female weighing 150 pounds can safely withstand up to nine hundred stings. Stings numbering fifteen hundred or more, however, can lead to death from liver and kidney failure.

If a person is highly allergic to bee venom, the above figures are meaningless, for just one sting could send him or her into anaphylactic shock, requiring immediate medical attention by trained professionals. People with allergies usually know who they are and carry an EpiPen or similar emergency kit containing injectable epinephrine along with chewable antihistamine tablets.

Happily, less than 1 percent of the U.S. population has true insect sting allergy. Stings account for about forty U.S. deaths each year, of which about seventeen can be attributed to honey bees. On average, one person every year dies after receiving many hundreds of stings from Africanized honey bees. Africanized bees (*Apis mellifera adansonii*) have claimed between one thousand and two thousand lives in Latin America since their accidental release near Sâo Paulo, Brazil, in 1957. In comparison, only ten people have died in the United States from Africanized bee stings since the bees' arrival from Mexico in 1994. You are at far greater risk of death while playing golf during a lightning storm or while riding in an automobile without wearing a seat belt.

There may be medical benefits attributable to bee venom. Some people actually solicit bee stings, placing bees against their skin and forcing them to sting. This may sound a bit masochistic, but the practice is called apitherapy, a sort of acupuncture using bees. No one is quite sure when or where it originated, but adherents believe it relieves the pain and reduces the disfigurement of rheumatoid arthritis, a crippling inflammatory disease of the joints. Justin Schmidt and other expert biomedical researchers believe that bee venom may in fact act as an anti-inflammatory agent. Certainly, there is promise here, and additional clinical studies are warranted.

There is a small commerical market for bee venom. It typically sells for $90,000 a pound, or $6,000 an ounce, and is mainly purchased by allergists who use it to test their patients for bee sting allergy. It's also used for venom desensitization. This procedure requires that ever-increasing amounts of bee venom be injected into allergic patients at regular intervals over a period of a year or more. The desensitization builds up antibodies to the venom in the patient's body, thereby protecting the person from risks of anaphylactic shock.

You might be wondering, How do they collect venom from bees? In the past, it was obtained by dissecting the bees' poison glands one at a time, a laborious process. In

1963, the technology was improved with the invention of a venom-collecting device by Charles Mraz and the late Roger Morse. It is a wooden board with a membrane covered by evenly spaced metal wires. This board is placed between two brood supers and the wires are electrified. This doesn't kill the bees, but the electric shock causes them to sting into the membrane. When removed, the venom is dried and scraped off the tough membrane. It took Charles Mraz thirty years to produce 6.6 pounds of pure, dried honey bee venom. He must have been a very patient man.

## How to Avoid Bee Attacks—
## and What to Do If You Get Stung

If you see lots of honey bees flying your way, remain calm. Walk toward shelter, preferably inside a house or vehicle with the windows rolled up. Don't move fast or flail your arms; that only alarms and excites the bees. Do not jump into a body of water. The bees will still be there when you come up for air. If you are nowhere near shelter, place a piece of light fabric over your face and head, ideally something that you can see through. The bees will try to sting your face and head, so this is the area that needs to be protected. Ducking into the neck of your shirt and pulling it up is a good defense. Holding your breath keeps bees from stinging your mouth and nose, since exhaled carbon dioxide is one of the cues that stimulates their stinging response.

If you are stung on your hand, put the hand in your

pocket. This may keep you from getting stung again. Each time a bee stings, it deposits a bit of alarm pheromone that smells like a ripe banana. (The odor comes from isopentyl acetate, which is one of the chemicals in ripe bananas—yes, bananas!) The alarm pheromone informs other bees where to sting. By the way, never eat a ripe banana next to a beehive.

Once you are out of danger, examine yourself for stings. If you see a small brown or black object in your skin, this is the stinger. Using a fingernail, the edge of a knife blade, or a credit card, carefully scrape it loose. Do not pinch the sting site, because that will force the venom deeper into the wound. If you can get the stinger out in less than a minute, chances are you will prevent much venom from entering your bloodstream. If possible, wash the sting site with soapy water. That removes the banana-scented "sting here" message left by a stinging bee. Normally, the pain of a sting will lessen after a few minutes. However, the sting site may start to itch a few hours later, and the itch might last a day or two. If within the first thirty minutes after being stung, you begin sweating profusely, have difficulty breathing, or experience blurred vision, get medical assistance immediately. These are the first warning signs of anaphylactic shock.

Large local site reactions following a bee or wasp sting are sometimes confused with anaphylactic shock. The fact is, in certain people, even one sting can result in redness, swelling, and itching far from the original sting site. For those people, a sting on a finger or wrist might result in a red, swollen, and painful arm up to the elbow. This reaction is scary, but it is not anaphylaxis and is not life-threatening.

## Bee Brood ("Honey, I Ate the Larvae")

Bee brood, or larvae, is featured on dinner menus in many parts of the world. But don't be shocked—it's perfectly safe and not bad-tasting. As I learned as a graduate student at UC Davis, tender white bee larvae make a delicious quiche. Bee larvae feed on pollen and honey and are probably more wholesome than some hormone-laced beef, pork, poultry, and fish (some with mercury) available in certain grocery stores. Bee larvae are also higher in protein and lower in fat than beef and, unlike grasshoppers, crickets, and other edible insects, don't have that annoying, indigestible chitinous cuticle (crunchy on the outside with a chewy center).

Bee brood as food actually has a long history. Earliest hunter-gatherers probably enjoyed larval bees straight from the comb. Modern honey hunters, including the Tongwe of Tanzania, the Shabanese of Congo, and the Kayapo of Brazil, all happily chew combs containing larval and pupal honey bees, which provide an important part of their annual protein intake. In Asian markets, combs of bee brood are commonly sold alongside honeycombs and bottled honey.

In the Canadian provinces of Manitoba, Saskatchewan, and Alberta, it was common for bee colonies to be killed in the winter, at the time of honey extraction. The colonies were then started anew with "package" bees sold for repopulation purposes. This represented a huge waste, not only of bees but also of the protein in their larvae. In 1960, Brian Hocking and Fumio Matsumara estimated that 132 tons of bee brood were lost when Canadian colonies were destroyed. They tried to develop a human market for bee brood, experimenting with both deep-fried larvae and baked larvae, cooked alone or in combination with other foods. Tasting panels preferred the deep-fried version, describing it as walnutlike in flavor and pork-crackling-like in texture. But the venture never got off the ground. People in the West are very squeamish about eating insects, and ingrained culinary habits and preferences are slow to change.

In Nepal, a bee brood dish called bakuti is a family favorite. It's made by squeezing brood combs through a woven mesh bag and collecting the milky juice. The liquid is gently heated for about five minutes while being constantly stirred. The result is similar in texture and flavor to scrambled eggs. In a taste test conducted in the United States, 85 percent of participants found bee brood à la Nepalese perfectly acceptable.

Bee larvae also make excellent pet food. Songbirds and reptiles are especially fond of it, and their owners would probably pay handsomely if supplies were regularly available. The beneficial-insects industry found that ladybird beetles and lacewings (beneficial insect predators that eat pests), normally difficult to raise in commercial insectaries, do very well on diets containing bee larvae. If you are an entrepreneurial beekeeper looking for alternative markets, maybe the pet food industry is just the right opportunity for you.

If fishing is your sport, honey bee larvae and pupae make dandy fish bait, just like the nest pests, wax worms (the caterpillars of wax moths), that consume beeswax and ruin combs for beekeepers everywhere.

# APPENDIX 3
# The Chemical Composition of Honey

| COMPONENT | AVERAGE | RANGE |
|---|---|---|
| Fructose/glucose ratio | 1.23 | 0.76–1.86 |
| Fructose (%) | 38.38 | 30.91–44.26 |
| Glucose (%) | 30.31 | 22.89–40.75 |
| Minerals (ash) | 0.169 | 0.02–1.03 |
| Moisture (%) | 17.2 | 13.4–22.9 |
| Reducing sugars (%) | 76.75 | 61.39–83.72 |
| Sucrose (%) | 1.31 | 0.25–7.57 |
| pH | 3.91 | |
| Total acidity (meq/kg) | 29.12 | 8.68–59.49 |
| True protein (mg/100g) | 168.6 | 57.7–567 |

Table from the National Honey Board, www.nhb.org/ foodtech/defdoc.html.

# APPENDIX 4
# Resources

## Mail Order Honeys

**A. G. Ferrari**
14234 Catalina Street
San Leandro, CA 94577
877-878-2783
www.agferrari.com
U.S. distributor of Sicilian and Tuscan honeys

**Bosque Honey Farms**
600 North Bosque Loop
Bosque Farms, NM 87068
505-869-2841
New Mexico raw honeys and bee pollen

**Burt's Bees, Inc.**
8221-A Brownleigh Drive
Raleigh, NC
www.burtsbees.com

**Candover Valley Honey Farm**
2, Hackwood Cottages
Alton Road
Basingstoke, Hampshire
England, RG21 32 BA
+44-1256-329064

**Cannon Bee Honey Company**
6105 11th Avenue South
Minneapolis, MN 55417
612-861-8999
Minnesota honeys, including basswood,
buckwheat, and clover

**Cowboy Honey Company**
P.O. Box 1387
Camp Verde, AZ 86322
520-567-3204
Arizona's famous mesquite honey

**Dean & Deluca**
2526 East 36th Street
Circle North
Wichita, KS 67219
877-826-9246
www.deandeluca.com
American, French, German, and Italian honeys

## Derwent Valley Apiaries

RSD 1268 Lyell Highway
New Norfolk, Tasmania 7140
+61-3-6261-1764
Tasmanian leatherwood honey

## Fauchon

442 Park Avenue (at 56th Street)
New York, NY 10022
212-308-5919
www.fauchon.com
Rare honeys

## Grossman Organic Farm

P.O. Box 1028
Tualatin, OR 97062
888-688-2582
Raw wildflower honeys and bee pollen from Oregon

## Guilmette's Busy Bees

5539 Noon Road
Bellingham, WA 98226
360-398-2146
Honey from the Pacific Northwest, including
fireweed, raspberry, and wildflower

**Harold P. Curtis Honey Company**
P.O. Box 1012
La Belle, FL 33975
Mangrove, orange blossom, and palmetto honeys
863-675-2187

**Hive Honey Shop**
93 Northcote Road
London SW11 6PL
+44-20-7924-6233
Various English honeys, honey condiments,
beauty products made with honey, and tableware

**Honey Garden Apiaries**
P.O. Box 189
Hinesburg, VT 05461
802-985-5852
Raw wildflower honeys from New York State and
Vermont, honey cough syrups, and beeswax candles

**Hunter's Honey Farm**
3440 Hancock Ridge Road
Martinsville, IN 46151
765-537-9430
Wildflower honeys from Indiana, beeswax candles,
and pollen

Marshall's Farm Natural Honey
P.O. Box 10880
Napa, CA 94581
800-624-4637
www.marshallshoney.com
Regional honeys from Napa Valley and
San Francisco Bay area

McEvoy Ranch
P.O. Box 341
Petaluma, CA 94953
707-769-4122
Lavender honey from Sonoma County

National Honey Board
390 Lashley Street
Longmont, CO 80501
303-776-2337
www.honey.com
Sources for honey: www.honeylocator.com

Plan Bee Honey
17 Van Dam Street
New York, NY 10013
212-627-0046
www.planbeehoney.com
Wildflower honeys from New York State,
comb honey, herb-infused honeys

**River Hill Bee Farm**
459 River Hill Road
Sparta, NC 28675
888-403-0392
www.riverhillhoney.com
Rare wildflower honeys, including sourwood
from the Blue Ridge Mountains

**Tropical Blossom Honey Company**
106 N. Ridgewood Avenue
Edgewater, FL 32132
386-428-9027
www.tropicbeehoney.com
Orange blossom honey from Florida, other
regional honeys, including palmetto and tupelo,
and flavored honeys

**Uvalde Honey**
P.O. Box 307
Uvalde, TX 78802
830-278-7078
Honey from acacia blossoms (huajillo)

# Craft and Hobby Supplies

GloryBee Foods, Inc.
P.O. Box 2744
Eugene, OR 97402
800-456-4923
www.glorybee.com
Beeswax candle making supplies, beekeeping equipment

# Beekeeping and Honey Bee Books

Avitable, A., and D. Sammataro. 1998. *The Beekeepers Handbook*, 3rd ed. Cornell University Press, Ithaca, NY.

Bonney, R. 1993. *Beekeeping: A Practical Guide*. Storey Books, Pownell, VT.

Bonney, R. 1991. *Hive Management: A Seasonal Guide for Beekeepers*. Storey Books, Pownell, VT.

Buchmann, S., and G. Nabhan. 1997. *The Forgotten Pollinators*. Island Press, Washington, D.C.

Flottam, K. (ed.). 1988. *The New Starting Right with Bees*, 21st ed. A. I. Root Company, Medina, OH.

Graham, J. M. 1992. *The Hive and the Honey Bee*. Dadant and Sons, Hamilton, IL.

Jacobsen, R. 2008. *Fruitless Fall: The Collapse of the Honey Bee and the Coming Agricultural Crisis*. Bloomsbury USA, New York, NY.

Longgood, W. 1985. *The Queen Must Die: And Other Affairs of Bees and Men*. W. W. Norton & Company, New York.

Morse, R. (ed.). 1990. *The ABC and XYZ of Bee Culture,* 40th ed. A. I. Root Company, Medina, OH.

Morse, R. 1986. *The Complete Guide to Beekeeping,* 3rd ed. E. P. Dutton, New York.

Morse, R. 1983. *A Year in the Beeyard.* Charles Scribner's Sons, New York.

Tautz, J. 2008. *The Buzz About Bees: Biology of a Superorganism.* Springer-Verlag, Berlin, Germany. Translated by Dr. David C. Sandeman.

## Beekeeping Journals

American Bee Journal
Dadant and Sons, Inc.
51 South 2nd Street
Hamilton, IL 62341
800-637-7468
www.dadant.com

Bee Culture
A. I. Root Company
623 West Liberty Street
Medina, OH 44256
800-289-7668
www.beeculture.com

# Honey Processing and
# Beekeeping Equipment

To find local beekeeping clubs, try:
www.bee.airoot.com/beeculture/who.html.

### 3B Sales & Service
P.O. Box 6054
North Logan, UT 84341
435-258-2009
3bsales&service@pcu.net

### A. I. Root Company
623 West Liberty Street
Medina, OH 44256
800-289-7668
www.rootcandles.com

### Bee Maid Honey
625 Roseberry Street
Winnipeg, Manitoba
Canada R2H 0T4
204-783-2240

### Better Bee, Inc.
8 Meader Road
Greenwich, NY 13834
800-632-3379

**Brushy Mountain Bee Farm**
610 Bethany Church Road
Moravian Falls, NC 28654
800-233-7929
www.beeequipment.com

**Dadant and Sons, Inc.**
51 South 2nd Street
Hamilton, IL 62341
800-637-7468
www.dadant.com

**Entomo-Logic**
Evan Sugden
21323 232nd Street SE
Monroe, WA 98272-8982
360-863-8547
den@seanet.com
www.seanet.com/~entomologic/entomologic_home.htmleasug

**Garvin Honey Company**
Pennine Bee Farm
Ellel, Lancaster
United Kingdom LA2 0QY
+44-1524-751347
www.garvinhoney.co.uk

**GloryBee Foods, Inc.**
P.O. Box 2744
Eugene, OR 97402
800-456-4923
www.glorybee.com

**Hector's Apiaries Services**
2297 Stanislaws Court
Santa Rosa, CA 95401
707-579-9416

**International Pollination, Inc.**
International Pollination Systems
Dr. Ron Bitner
16645 Plum Lane
Caldwell, ID 83605
208-454-0086
www.pollination.com

**Judi's Farm Market**
8020 Steveston Highway
Richmond, British Columbia
Canada, V7A 1M3
604-275-9535

Kidd Bros. Produce Ltd.
5312 Grimmer Street
Burnaby, British Columbia
Canada, V5H 2H2
604-437-9757

Knox Cellars
Brian Griffin
1607 Knox Avenue
Bellingham, WA 98225
360-733-3283
Sales@knoxcellars.com
Brian@knoxcellars.com
www.knoxcellars.com

Mann Lake Ltd.
501 S. First Street
Hackensack, MN 56452
800-233-6663
www.mannlakeltd.com

Maxant Industries, Inc.
P.O. Box 453-S
Ayer, MA 01432
978-772-0576

Pollinator Paradise
Karen Strickler
31140 Circle Drive
Parma, ID 83660
solitary@pollinatorparadise.com
www.pollinatorparadise.com

Ruhl Bee Supply
12713 NE Whitaker Way
Portland, OR 97230
503-256-4231

Western Bee Supplies, Inc.
P.O. Box 190
Polson, MT 59860
800-548-8440
www.westernbee.com

## Sources of Native Bees (Non-Apis) and Solitary Bee Nests

Custom Paper Tubes, Inc.
P.O. Box 44187
Cleveland, OH 44144-0187
216-362-2964
800-343-8823
beetubes@custompapertubes.com
www.custompapertubes.com

Hunter's Mason Bees
14313 NE 177th Court
Woodinville, WA 98072
206-851-1263
http://huntersmasonbees.com

## Join the Pollinator Partnership!
## (www.pollinator.org; www.nappc.org)

The Pollinator Partnership, and its North American Pollinator Protection Campaign, may be just the resource you've been looking for. Whether you are fact-finding for a school report, growing a pollinator-friendly garden, or just want to learn something cool about pollinators, this is the Web site for you and your family. When you enter your zip code, you can read or download a colorful Ecoregional Planting Guide customized to where you live. The guide has great ideas about which flowers to plant and which types of pollinating animals you can attract and watch. There's information in three languages (English, French, and Spanish) because the partnership includes members in the United States, Canada, and Mexico.

I am a founding member of this nonprofit conservation organization, which was started in 1999. Although we support beekeepers and provide lots of honey bee information, our mission is to conserve and help all pollinators (native bees, ants, wasps, beetles, flies, butterflies, moths, hummingbirds, and nectar bats). We have more than 120 federal agency partners, nongovernmental organizations, corporations, and individuals working to preserve and protect pollinators and their plants. Look for our activities and programs near you. Each year, we promote grassroots events (lectures, hikes, hands-on demos, contests) during National Pollinator Week, always celebrated during the last week in June. The Pollinator Partnership prints and distributes a gorgeous full-color pollinator/plant poster used in hundreds of schools, nature centers, and homes. Get your poster and spread the word that honey bees and other pollinators are in trouble and need our help.

# Sources

## Introduction

Fellow entomologist Edward O. Wilson of Harvard University has influenced my thinking and writing perhaps more than anyone else. It has been my pleasure to join him on ant-collecting trips into the "sky island" mountaintop regions of southern Arizona.

Kellert, S. R. 1997. *Kinship to Mastery: Biophilia in Human Evolution and Development.* Island Press, Washington, DC.

Kellert, S. R., and E. O. Wilson (eds.). 1993. *The Biophilia Hypothesis.* Island Press, Washington, DC.

Pyle, R. M. 1993. *The Thunder Tree: Lessons from an Urban Wildland.* Houghton Mifflin Co., Boston, MA.

Wilson, E. O. 2002. *The Future of Life.* Alfred A. Knopf, New York.

Wilson, E. O. 1996. *In Search of Nature.* Island Press, Washington, DC.

Wilson, E. O. 1992. *The Diversity of Life.* Belknap Press, Cambridge, MA.

Wilson, E. O. 1984. *Biophilia: The Human Bond with*

*Other Species*. Harvard University Press, Cambridge, MA.

Wilson, E. O. 1975. *Sociobiology: The New Synthesis*. Belknap Press, Cambridge, MA.

Wilson, E. O. 1971. *The Insect Societies*. Belknap Press, Cambridge, MA.

## Chapter 1. Secrets of the Bee;
## Chapter 2. Flowers and Bees: The Dance;
## Chapter 3. A Year in the Life
## of a Beekeeper

Descriptions of the life and seasons of the beekeeper are found in books by Sue Hubbell and Douglas Whynott, and in *The Queen Must Die,* an often overlooked but essential work by the late William Longgood. I also suggest *The Hive and the Honey Bee* and *The ABC and XYZ of Bee Culture,* especially for new beekeepers.

Crane, E. 1990. *Bees and Beekeeping: Science, Practice and World Resources,* Cornell University Press, Ithaca, NY.

Graham, J. (ed.). 1992. *The Hive and the Honey Bee*. Dadant and Sons, Hamilton, IL.

Hubbell, S. 1988. *A Book of Bees*. Random House, New York.

Hubbell, S. 1986. *A Country Year*. Random House, New York.

Kelly, K. 1995. *Out of Control: The New Biology of*

*Machines, Social Systems, and the Economic World.* Addison-Wesley, Reading, MA.

Longgood, W. 1985. *The Queen Must Die: And Other Affairs of Bees and Men.* W. W. Norton, New York.

Morse, R. A. (ed.). 1990. *The ABC and XYZ of Bee Culture,* 40th ed. A. I. Root, Medina, OH.

Morse, R. A. 1986. *The Complete Guide to Beekeeping,* 3rd ed. E. P. Dutton, New York.

Morse, R. A., and T. Hooper (eds.). 1985. *The Illustrated Encyclopedia of Beekeeping.* Alphabooks, Sherborne, UK.

Whynott, D. 1991. *Following the Bloom: Across America with the Migratory Beekeepers.* Stackpole Books, Harrisburg, PA.

## Chapter 4. Staying in Touch: The Beekeeper's Craft

The books by Dr. Eva Crane and Hilda Ransome are good introductions to the history of beekeeping. The articles by Donald Brand and the Weavers will introduce you to the fascinating world of meliponiculture, the keeping of stingless bees by ancient and modern Maya.

Berenbaum, M. R. 1995. *Bugs in the System: Insects and Their Impact on Human Affairs.* Addison-Wesley, Reading, MA.

Brand, D. D. 1988. "The Honey Bee in New Spain and Mexico." *Journal of Cultural Geography* 9, no. 1: 71–82.

Crane, E. 1992. "The Past and Present Status of Bee-keeping with Stingless Bees." *Bee World* 73, no. 1: 29–42.

Crane, E. 1990. *Bees and Beekeeping: Science, Practice and World Resources*. Cornell University Press, Ithaca, NY.

Crane, E. 1983. *The Archaeology of Beekeeping*. Gerald Duckworth, London.

Ransome, H. M. 1937. *The Sacred Bee in Ancient Times and Folklore*. George Allen & Unwin, London.

Virgil. 1982. *Georgics,* trans. L. P. Wilkinson. Penguin Books, New York.

Weaver, N., and E. C. Weaver. 1981. "Beekeeping with the stingless bee, Melipona beecheii, by the Yucatecan Maya." *Bee World* 62, no. 1: 7–19.

## Chapter 5. The Beginning of an Enduring Passion: Prehistoric Honey Hunters

The books by Dr. Eva Crane are wells of information on prehistoric rock art depicting ancient honey hunts. We thank Eva for allowing us to reproduce some of the evocative illustrations found in these works. The 1937 book by Hilda Ransome, now out of print, contains unique facts about bees and honey in the ancient world that aren't found anywhere else.

Crane, E. 2001. *The Rock Art of Honey Hunters*. International Bee Research Association. Cardiff, Wales.

Crane, E. 1983. *The Archaeology of Beekeeping*. International Bee Research Association, Cardiff, Wales.

Ransome, H. M. 1937. *The Sacred Bee in Ancient Times and Folklore*. George Allen & Unwin, London.

## Chapter 6. A Taste of Honey: Sampling Varieties from Around the World

The recent books by Stephanie Rosenbaum and Sue Style provide an excellent entrée into the world of boutique honeys, monofloral sources, and exciting varietals. The Web site of the National Honey Board is also a great place to learn about different honeys and where to buy them. See Appendix 4 for other sources of both common and rare honeys.

Crane, E. (ed.). 1975. *Honey: A Comprehensive Survey*. Crane, Russak, NY.

Rosenbaum, S. 2002. *Honey: From Flower to Table*. Chronicle Books, San Francisco.

Style, S. 1993. *Honey: From Hive to Honeypot*. Chronicle Books, San Francisco.

## Chapter 7. Trading Honey in the Ancient and Modern Worlds

Good sources on the honey trade include, once again, the works of Dr. Eva Crane and Donald Brand.

Brand, D. D. 1988. "The Honey Bee in New Spain and Mexico." *Journal of Cultural Geography* 9, no. 1: 71–82.

Crane, E. 1980. *A Book of Honey*. Oxford University Press, Oxford, UK.

Crane, E. (ed.). 1975. *Honey: A Comprehensive Survey*. Crane, Russak, NY.

Toussaint-Samat, M. 1993. *History of Food*. Blackwell, Oxford, UK.

Virgil. 1982. *Georgics*, trans. L. P. Wilkinson. Penguin Books, New York.

Virgil. 1965. *Eclogues and Georgics*. J. M. Dent and Sons, London.

# Chapter 8. Searching for Gold: Ancient Rituals and Modern-Day Honey Hunters

I was moved by the words and images of Eric Valli and Diane Summers as they recorded, both in print and on film in a National Geographic television special, the adventures of Gurung honey hunters in the foothills of the Himalayas. The color photographs in their elegant book shouldn't be missed.

Buchmann, S. L., and G. P. Nabhan. 1997. *The Forgotten Pollinators*. Island Press, Washington, DC.

Crane, E. 1983. *The Archaeology of Beekeeping*. Gerald Duckworth, London.

Dollin, L. 2001. "Australian Native Bees—Treasured in

Aboriginal Heritage, Part 2." *Aussie Bee* 16: 15–17.
Australian Native Bee Research Centre, North Richmond NSW, Australia.

Dollin, L. 2000. "Australian Native Bees—Treasured in Aboriginal Heritage, Part 1." *Aussie Bee* 15: 10–12.
Australian Native Bee Research Centre, North Richmond NSW, Australia.

Dollin, L. 2000. "Overland Expedition for an Elusive Drone." *Aussie Bee* 15: 8–9. Australian Native Bee Research Centre, North Richmond NSW, Australia.

Dollin, L. 1997. "Exploring Western Australia—Part 2: An Old Native Bee Farming Area of the Aborigines." *Aussie Bee* 4: 14–15. Australian Native Bee Research Centre, North Richmond NSW, Australia.

Ransome, H. M. 1937. *The Sacred Bee in Ancient Times and Folklore*. George Allen & Unwin, London.

Valli, E., and D. Summers. 1988. *Honey Hunters of Nepal*. Harry N. Abrams, New York.

# Chapter 9. Good for What Ails You

It's wonderful that honey, always a popular folk medicine, is being evaluated and clinically tested by modern medical researchers. The pioneering work with manuka honey by Dr. Peter Molan of New Zealand and his colleagues is especially exciting.

Armstrong, S., and G. W. Otis. 1995. "The Antibacterial Properties of Honey." *Bee Culture* 123, no. 9: 500–2.

Beck, B. 1938. *Honey and Health*. Robert McBride, New York.

Breaste, J. H. 1930. *The Edwin Smith Surgical Papyrus*. University of Chicago Press, Chicago.

Guido, M. 1975. *The Healing Hand: Man and Wound in the Ancient World*. Harvard University Press, Cambridge, MA.

Han, H., G. E. Miller, and N. DeVille. 2003. *Ancient Herbs, Modern Medicine*. Bantam, New York.

Jarvis, D. C. 1958. *Folk Medicine*. Holt, Rinehart and Winston, New York.

Molan, P. C. 1999. "Why Honey Is Effective as a Medicine. 1. Its Use in Modern Medicine." *Bee World* 80, no. 2: 80–92.

Molan, P. C. 1999. "Potential of Honey in the Treatment of Wounds and Burns." *American Journal of Clinical Dermatology* 2, no. 1: 13–19.

Molan, P. C. 1998. "A Brief Review of Honey as a Clinical Dressing." *Primary Intention* 6, no. 4: 148–58.

Molan, P. C. 1992. "The Antibacterial Activity of Honey. 1. The Nature of the Antibacterial Activity." *Bee World* 73, no. 1: 528.

Molan, P. C. 1992. "The Antibacterial Activity of Honey. 2. Variation in the Potency of the Antibacterial Activity." *Bee World* 73, no. 2: 59–76.

Munn, P., and R. Jones (eds.). 2001. *Honey and Healing*. International Bee Research Association, Cardiff, Wales.

Traynor, J. 2002. *Honey: The Gourmet Medicine*. Kovak Books, Bakersfield, CA.

## Chapter 10. How Sweet It Is: Cooking with Honey Through the Ages

One of the best histories of cooking with honey is Maguelonne Toussaint-Samat's *History of Food*. Harold McGee's book is an entertaining and informative account of cooking with honey today.

Brothwell, D., and P. Brothwell. 1969. *Food in Antiquity*. Frederick A. Praeger, New York.

Corriher, S. 1997. *Cookwise*. William Morrow, New York.

McGee, H. 1984. *On Food and Cooking*. Scribner, New York.

Roden, C. 1996. *A Book of Jewish Food*. Alfred A. Knopf, New York.

Rosenbaum, S. 2002. *Honey: From Flower to Table*. Chronicle Books, San Francisco.

Style, S. 1993. *Honey: From Hive to Honeypot*. Chronicle Books, San Francisco.

Tannahill, R. 1989. *Food in History*. Crown, New York.

Toussaint-Samat, M. 1993. *History of Food*. Blackwell, Oxford, UK.

Witty, H. 1997. *The Good Stuff Cookbook*. Workman, New York.

# Photo/Illustration Credits

Pages 3, 7, 8, 19, 20, 24, 87, 96, 149: Stephen Buchmann

Page 29: Division of Agriculture and National Resources, University of California, Davis.

Page 48: Tony Sagrillo

Page 52: Crane, Eva. 1983. *The Archeology of Beekeeping.* Cornell University Press, Ithaca, NY. Courtesy of Gerald Duckworth & Co.

Page 56: Museo de America, Madrid

Pages 61, 62: Crane, Eva (ed.). 2001. *The Rock Art of Honey Hunters.* International Bee Research Association, Cardiff, UK.

Pages 103, 105, 110: Paul Mirocha

# Recipe Permissions

Page 140: National Honey Board

Pages 141, 142: Kimberly Larson

# INDEX

Page numbers in *italics* refer to illustrations.

# About the Author

STEPHEN BUCHMANN is a beekeeper and an associate professor of entomology at the University of Arizona in Tucson. He served on a National Academy of Sciences committee on the status of pollinators in North America and is a founding member of the Pollinator Partnership. He coauthored two nonfiction adult titles, *The Forgotten Pollinators* and *Letters from the Hive: An Intimate History of Bees, Honey, and Humankind*, and a children's picture book, *The Bee Tree*. He served as scientific advisor for the upcoming Disneynature film *Hidden Beauty*, about bees, other pollinators, and flowers. Besides working on new books, he is currently filming and directing a documentary on the Yucatán peninsula in Mexico about the Maya and their sacred beecraft. For fun, Stephen explores the world with camera and tripod, then creates inkjet prints of favorite images. He lives in the Sonoran Desert, in Tucson.